Making Twig
Garden Furniture

ALSO BY ABBY RUOFF

Making Twig Furniture & Household Things
Making Rustic Originals

Making Twig Garden Furniture

ABBY RUOFF

Photographs by ABBY RUOFF

Illustrations by SIA KASKAMANIDIS
& EDWARD R. TURNER

Hartley
&Marks
PUBLISHERS

Published by

HARTLEY & MARKS PUBLISHERS INC.

P. O. Box 147   3661 West Broadway
Point Roberts, WA   Vancouver, BC
98281   V6R 2B8

LIBRARY OF CONGRESS CATALOGING-IN-PUBLICATION DATA
Ruoff, Abby.
   Making twig garden furniture / Abby Ruoff ; photographs by Abby Ruoff;
illustrations by Sia Kaskamanidis.—2nd ed.
      p. cm.
   ISBN 0-88179-186-5 (alk. paper)
   1. Outdoor furniture. 2. Furniture making. 3. Twig furniture. I. Title.

TT197.5.O9 R86 2001
684.1'8—dc21   2001024189

Design & composition by The Typeworks
Set in MINION, POETICA CHANCERY, & SCALA SANS

Printed in the U.S.A.

TO BENJAMIN AND SAMUEL

Children are like flowers in a garden;
tend to them and nurture them, and
they will grow strong and beautiful.
— MY GRANDMOTHER

Acknowledgments

I want to express my appreciation to Sue Tauber for planting the first seeds, and to Vic Marks, for his faith in this project. I wish also to thank Susan Juby, my editor, who told me from the beginning that she was "familiar with my work," and waited patiently until every last word was written, and to Annalisa Taylor, Hartley & Marks' promotions coordinator, who has faith in my ability to articulate.

I would like to thank my neighbors who invited me into their gardens: Kristine Flones of Whittenberg, Leza of Woodstock, Gerry Jacobs of Easton Lane, and Malcolm Rose of Bearsville.

To Carl, my husband, who taught me the language of the forest and encouraged me to write this book, I am forever grateful.

Contents

Grandfather's Planting Twigs

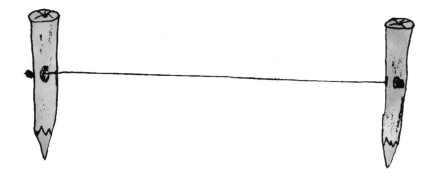

A homemade gardening aid,
remarkable in its simplicity and usefulness.

Whittle the ends of two 12" long, ¾" diameter twigs; drill a
hole through each twig 3" down from the top; thread six yards of
strong twine through both holes, and knot the ends.

Use like a compass to lay out circles and arcs,
or measure and divide straight lines.

Introduction

The Cedar Gate   Tannersville, N. Y.

THEY ARE SIMPLE THINGS. A trellis. A bird feeder. A chair. But look again, and these simple pieces are practical and ingenious: green willow shoots are shaped into arches to support climbing vines; a hollow white birch log holds a supply of bird seed; and a few forked branches are nailed together to form a chair. Twig furniture and gardens are natural partners, throwbacks to a simpler time, and all the things we love: a rose-covered arbor, a fence of woven willow shoots to border and divide the salad greens, a scarecrow formed of sticks and twigs to guard the corn, a mixture of country memories and lazy summer afternoons. Of the wide range of garden and outdoor furnishings available today, made of everything from cast iron to stone, nothing seems better suited to the garden than pieces fashioned from branches, bark, and vines. The simple charm of a natural seat tucked in the garden reflects the best of a rustic tradition; here the beauty of field, forest, and garden embrace.

In the late 1800s the creation of grand and glorious gardens became a colorful way of displaying prosperity, and the wealthy became preoccupied with garden ornament. The Victorian era, and its romanticized vision of nature, created the perfect setting for rustic work, and landscape designers began to place seats of twisted, gnarled rhododendron and laurel in unexpected corners and along curving paths. Soon the Golden Age of rustic garden furnishings gave way to the more practical side of the gardener's nature, and simple bean poles, tomato supports, rose trellises, and arbors were fashioned out of available twigs. Today increased environmental awareness finds more people moving their lifestyles out of doors. Not only are they eating and entertaining on the porch or in the garden, but very often they are growing their own pesticide-free produce. As garden activity grows, so too does the popularity of garden furnishings. Soon after the publication of my first rustic twig book, *Making Twig Furniture*, 1991, many readers wrote requesting plans for rustic designs to be used in the garden, such as trellis work, arbors, and fanciful birdhouses and feeders. This book is a direct result of those requests.

Designing these rustic furnishings has rekindled happy childhood memories of gardens where twigs were used to stake giant sunflowers, and helped to support vined beans and peas. I remember with fondness attaching short branches to empty seed packages to mark the tidy rows in my grandfather's vegetable garden. Every year, as sure as spring turns to summer, my grandmother's flower garden rose up under the ancient lilacs. The same twig bench remained tucked into a clearing between the day lilies and the phlox in all seasons. That bench, wobbly though it was, served as a special place for childhood dreams. I think it was here that I first saw the connection between the tree and the furniture. The bench had remained in the same spot for so many years that it seemed to grow right out of the ground. The magic of its creation fascinated me, and rustic furniture became part of my earliest memories.

Gardeners and craftspeople share a common bond. The creative challenges are the same whether you are laying out plants in a landscape, or designing a chair. There is something very fulfilling about working with your hands. The personal expression that helps to make a garden great is part of the same creative energy that builds rustic twig furnishings. Various demands on my time have forced me to neglect my own gardens for several years, but now as a result of these new projects I have expanded my herb garden and flower beds. In truth, I cannot tell if the garden is a backdrop for the furniture, or the furniture is the reason for the garden. Sometimes in my dreams, waking or sleeping, I think I have recaptured the details of that crudely nailed together bench in grandmother's garden where I spent so many happy summer hours.

Outdoor furnishings, like their indoor counterparts, require a sense of belonging or purpose. It is important to consider dimensions and scale when placing outdoor furnishings, for it is the total arrangement that creates the beautiful garden. Center a pedestal sundial in a herb garden, hang a window box on a kitchen garden fence, or position trelliage along a brick city wall or weathered barn for a distinctive display. A few well-chosen rustic garden twig elements will help turn any outdoor area into a cozy retreat, and learning to make twig garden furnishings is easier than you think.

Remember, interesting and appealing areas are created when ingenuity and resourcefulness take precedence. Use this book as a guide—fine tune your creativity and educate your eyes to make something wonderful out of twigs and branches.

There are projects here for every skill level—beginner, intermediate, or experienced—and they are varied enough to interest and challenge any craftsperson.

Note that the pattern pieces need to be enlarged on a photocopier, and that several pieces need to be enlarged by more than 200%, which is beyond the capacity of most copiers, so they will need to be enlarged twice.

Your local copy shop should be able to do your enlargements if you don't have access to a machine.

CHAPTER 1

Finding the Wood

RUSTIC GARDEN FURNITURE DESIGNS are dictated by the character of the wood they are made from, so it is important to be able to identify various trees and shrubs and to familiarize yourself with their individual characteristics. Since not all trees are available in all regions or climates, I encourage you to experiment with your local materials. You will also want to learn various cultivating techniques to avoid destroying existing stands so they are preserved for future generations.

For the purposes of this book, you should know that trees are single-stemmed plants that attain a height of at least 15 ft., while shrubs are often multi-stemmed and generally grow to about 10 ft. Twigs are young limbs, called shoots when they are new growth, and are usually not more than two inches in diameter. Learning to recognize species under various growing conditions is not always easy. Many trees that grow at high elevations on mountains are twisted and sprawling as a result of a short growing season and strong winds, but at low levels they stand tall and straight. When searching for wood, you should carry a tree identification manual to help you recognize trees by their leaves, flowers, fruits, and bark.

A very good manual for tree identification is the series by the Nature Study Guild, Box 972, Berkeley, Calif., 94701. Send for their catalog for your area, such as *Pacific Coast Tree Finder*, *Rocky Mountain Tree Finder*, *Desert Tree Finder*, or *Winter Tree Finder*. These are small manuals that can be kept in your pocket or in the glove compartment of your car. Other helpful manuals are *The Simon and Schuster Pocket Guide to Trees, Trees and Shrubs (Northeastern and Central North America)*, and *The Peterson Field Guide Series*.

COLLECTING TWIGS AND BRANCHES

If you do not own your own "back 40" country acres where you can gather twigs and limbs, here are some lessons in creative harvesting. One woman who lives in a small city told me she befriended the park workers in the city park. As they prune trees, they save some of the longer branches for her. She rewards them at holidays with homemade pies, and now has several twig chairs and baskets in her apartment. I do not want to tell you to wish for a calamity, but a friend of mine in Iowa recently experienced a dreadful ice storm, with tree branches breaking off under the weight of the ice. While his neighbors were bemoaning the loss of favorite trees, he was busy gathering twigs for future projects. Be alert for innovative ways to secure your materials. Fruit orchards, such as apple, pear, or cherry, can be another good source of materials. Search out sites where developers and builders are working in your area. All too often such commercial ventures will destroy precious natural resources. Although this is heartbreaking, you can put the cut trees to good use, rather than seeing them wasted in a burning pit. I have even heard about someone who approached a builder to obtain some cut trees, and was offered pay to cart them away. Now there is an agreeable situation! Friendly farmers or loggers might be glad to sell you a small amount of twigs and limbs for a nominal charge. There are many innovative ways to obtain materials, and if you are enterprising I know you will succeed.

How to Choose and Gather Twigs

Always select fresh materials. Cut the twigs with care and be sure you don't pull the roots out. If you are collecting thin branches, such as willow, leave more than you remove, so that you preserve the plant and are assured a plentiful future supply. Use only sharp cutting tools (axes, saws, or clippers), and never rip or tear the branches, as this can destroy a living plant. Examine the twigs for insects or larvae, and try to avoid any pests. If these seem to be a problem, treat the wood with a safe garden insecticide before building your furniture.

How to Examine the Twigs for Larvae

When you are gathering twigs and poles, take time to check for insect activity, since you will not want to build furniture out of infested wood. Wood-eating insects on living trees are relatively rare. Most wood eaters feed on dead trees. If your cut wood supply is kept outside for a prolonged period, it will become a target for bugs. Examine the branches for tiny holes or deep channels. This is not necessarily a sure-fire method for detecting live insects, but it is a clue for further investigation. If you suspect that a branch is infested, separate it from the rest of your supply for a week, and check it daily. If you find small piles of sawdust around or near the holes, the limb should be discarded.

Watch for twig-boring insects when you are harvesting thin twigs and vines. The larvae of beetles often bore through tender twigs and small branches, killing large portions of a tree's crown. When you are out collecting twigs, remember to look up. Learn to recognize the signs of tree damage.

If you find signs of insect activity after your piece is built, you will have to spray it with an insecticide. Several safe, effective insecticides are available today, and more are being developed. Check with your local nursery or hardware store, and make sure the product you choose is safe for indoor and outdoor use. You should use a product that is made with a natural *botanical pyrethrin* base, for pieces that will be used outside. Be sure to read the label carefully. It is always best to apply the insecticide outdoors.

ALDER

Eight species of native alder grow rapidly in North America, often forming thickets in moist soil. All alder trees have irregularly toothed, prominently veined, oval or oblong leaves. The red alder tree of the Pacific Northwest often reaches heights of 30 to 40 ft., and the outside edges of its leaves are rolled under. The white alder, although usually smaller, is similar to the red alder, except that its leaves are flat. The Sitka alder is distinctive because of its smooth grey-green bark, covered with warty clusters. The undersides of its outermost leaves are glossy and sticky. The thin leaf alder and the mountain alder have oblong leaves, two to three inches wide, with orange-brown midribs that sport rusty brown hairs. The undersides of its leaves are dull, not sticky. The Arizona alder, which grows in the southwestern United States, has slightly smaller leaves with a yellow midrib and a smooth, grey to brownish bark. The seaside alder, on the other hand, grows on the east coast. With its round-topped crown of zigzag branches, it is quite easy to identify.

The alder is a relatively obscure tree, and it is often overlooked as a viable wood for twig furnishings. However, as a close cousin to birch and hazelnut, its pliable branches are invaluable. Alder can be used to make trellises and fences, and to form the backs on garden chairs. Larger pieces can be used for the garden gate.

Where Alder Trees Grow

Most alder grows in the western regions of the United States and Canada. It is easily distinguishable in the spring, when staminate catkins cast a distinctive greenish-brown hue over the surrounding area. Alder is found around lakes, along streams and creek beds, and in open swamps.

BEECH

There are almost 100 species of beech native to North America. They are handsome, deciduous trees with short-stemmed, prominently veined, elliptical leaves, three to six inches long. Their smooth bark is blue-grey and commonly blotched with dark grey speckling and thin split lines. On older beech trees a smoky, dark tone is often noticeable on one side of the trunk, with still darker areas around the base. Young beech trees are easily recognizable by their deep red-brown buds, covered with cream-colored flecks.

Beech wood is tight-grained, heavy, and strong. Because the bark on beech trees is strong and tight, it does not peel off easily, making it particularly desirable for making twig chairs and plant stands.

Where Beech Trees Grow

Beech trees are usually found in deep forests, surrounded by oaks or maples. They grow from southern Ontario to Nova Scotia, from central Wisconsin to Maine, and south to Texas and northern Florida.

BIRCH

While you'll find information on white paper birch in Bark and Vine Projects in chapter 2, there are many other useful birches growing throughout most of North America. One of them is the low-growing Alaskan shrub called ground birch, which is an important summer food for northern animals. Yellow birch yields bark that is yellowish to bronze, which peels into thin, narrow strips. Water birch is a small, slender tree, often with drooping branches and a dark brown bark. River birch has a scaly, grey-black trunk on older trees, and thin, pinkish bark on young trees. The river birch's trunk is often divided into multi-arched limbs, while the blueleaf birch grows most commonly as a shrub, with a rosy-hued bark that does not peel. Yukon birch is a stately tree that often reaches heights of 25 ft. It can be identified by its dark brown bark and white lenticel clusters (ventilating pores in the bark). Black birch is set apart from the other birches with its mahogany-red bark, smooth and glossy in young trees, and rough and scaly in older trees. Its leaves and bark have a sweet, minty aroma, and it is sometimes called sweet birch. Birch leaves vary in shape, but all have prominent veins and short leaf stems.

The strength of birch and the coloring of its bark make it very desirable for furniture. Its sturdy limbs are useful for shelves, planters, birdhouses, and feeders.

Where Birch Trees Grow

Birch trees grow rapidly, often forming extensive forests in the north. Yellow and black birch grow along the east coast, from northern Canada into the United States as far south as Georgia. Water birch and Yukon birch grow in the western United States and Canada. River birch is the only native birch that grows at low elevations, along streams in the southeastern United States. Blueleaf birch is found in Maine and eastern Quebec, along the St. Lawrence River valley. Its blue-green leaves make it easy to identify.

BOX ELDER

The box elder has three-leaflet leaves with jagged edges, similar to maple leaves. Its bark is pastel red, purple, or bright green, often coated with a thin white haze. Box elder branches are brittle when dry, so it may be helpful to soak them in a bucket of water until ready for use. These colorful and glossy twigs are suitable for small projects such as the hanging herb and flower drying rack.

Where Box Elder Trees Grow

Box elder grows in the western United States, from Illinois to Colorado and northern Texas up to the Pacific Northwest. It is an extremely adaptable tree, growing on high or low ground, in sunlight or shade, in moist or dry areas.

CEDAR

Most cedar wood is aromatic, including some cypress and juniper. Cedar foliage is compact and dark with a slightly prickly texture. Incense cedars are covered with dark brown, deeply furrowed bark. Northern white cedar and Atlantic white cedar also have deeply furrowed barks, ranging in color from ash-grey to reddish-brown. Western red cedar is distinguishable by its vertically ridged, brownish-grey, shredded bark. Port Orford cedar has dark green foliage similar to the Western red cedar's, but the scales on its branches are tighter. Alaska cedar is a smaller tree with yellow-green foliage and a rougher texture than the Port Orford. It usually has grey shaggy bark and thin scales. Its interior wood is most often yellow in appearance.

Sturdy cedar limbs were used for the Cedar and Vine Garden Bench. Their shaggy bark adds texture and interest to any project. Cedar poles are especially useful where strong supports are required, such as the summer house.

Where Cedar Trees Grow

Cedar in one form or another is plentiful throughout most of the United States and Canada. It is found alongside water bodies from North Dakota to Maine and southern Ontario, and then south to central Texas and northern Florida. In the northwest, throughout Oregon, Washington, and British Columbia, cedars of various types grow in abundance. Its shaggy bark, remarkable shape, and unique aroma make it easy to locate.

CHERRY

Cherry trees grow in abundance throughout most parts of the northern hemisphere, often in cool regions. Black cherry is usually easy to identify because of its distinctive color. In the sapling stage, its bark is smooth and reddish-brown, turning dark grey and flaky on mature trees. All cherry trees have simple, alternating leaves that are two to five inches long, a bit leathery, and serrated along their edges.

The strength and beautiful coloring of the young cherry saplings make them ideal for twig chair parts. The wood is usually free from warping, but should be well seasoned before it is used because it shrinks during seasoning.

Where Cherry Trees Grow

Cherry trees of one type or another are common throughout most of North America. The black cherry grows in rich soils and woods from southeastern Manitoba to Nova Scotia, and from eastern South Dakota to Maine and south to eastern Texas and central Florida.

The pin cherry grows 15 to 25 ft. tall, and is found across most of Canada to Nova Scotia, and as far south as South Carolina to the east and Utah in the west.

The common chokecherry is a shrub or small tree found in most of North America, except in the extreme southern areas of Texas, Arkansas, Louisiana,

Alabama, Georgia, and Florida. It can grow 25 ft. tall and up to eight inches in diameter. The chokecherry has white flowers in the spring, and tiny, dark red cherries in the summer, usually about one-third of an inch in diameter.

The bitter cherry has red to black cherries, about half an inch in diameter. Distinguishable by its brownish bark with horizontal, orange lenticels, it can grow to 40 ft. and 18 inches in diameter. The bitter cherry occurs along the western half of North America—from British Columbia and Alberta throughout most of Washington and Oregon—and as far east and south as parts of Nevada and Arizona.

Hollyleaf cherry has egg-shaped, evergreen leaves, one to two inches long and an inch wide. Along with the rare Catalina cherry, it grows along the extreme western coast of California.

BALD CYPRESS

The bald cypress, also known as southern or red cypress, can grow to grand heights of 100 ft. It has yellow-green needles that turn brown before falling in the autumn. Bald cypress also produces wrinkled cones about an inch wide that mature in one season. Its branches are often draped with Spanish moss.

Bald cypress forms "knees," which are really branches that grow out of its widespread underground root system. These sharp, pointed extensions project above the surface. Craftspeople often use these "knees" to create lamp bases and sculptures.

Bald cypress is most often used to build chairs, loveseats, and planters. Its naturally pale bark is beautiful left in its natural state, and looks lovely indoors or on covered porches. Cypress will weather to a soft grey. Left outside for a season, your weathered cypress piece will be appreciated for its subtle coloring.

Where Cypress Trees Grow

The bald cypress is probably familiar to those who live along the southern part of the United States. It grows in large forests, especially in the wet coastal plains of Florida. Although not all bald cypress grows in water, it is abundant where periodic flooding is common. Most often associated with rustic work from Florida, the species has a large growing area, ranging from southern

New Jersey to Florida, along the Atlantic Coastal Plain, across the Gulf Coast Lowlands into Texas and Mexico, and up the Mississippi basin as far as Illinois and Indiana.

EUCALYPTUS (BLUE GUM)

Eucalyptus bark is usually thin and reddish-brown in color. It peels off in long strips, revealing a creamy-white or grey underbark. Its leathery curved leaves are pale green, 6 to 12 inches long, with a sharp tip. The blue gum can grow to heights of 200 ft.

Eucalyptus benefits from frequent pruning, and 10-year-old trees can provide a continuous supply of branches useful for chair parts, and a variety of other twig projects.

Where Eucalyptus Trees Grow

The branches and bark of over 200 species of Australian eucalyptus trees are widely used in constructing twig furniture. In North America, the blue gum eucalyptus is generally found on the western border of California, south to Arizona and New Mexico, stretching along the Gulf Coast of Texas, and east to Florida. Because of its capacity to grow in semi-arid regions, blue gum eucalyptus has been widely planted for windbreaks along dry fields.

GOLDEN CHINKAPIN (GOLDEN LEAF CHESTNUT)

The golden chinkapin has leathery, oblong, evergreen leaves, two to five inches long, with smooth curled margins. Its flowers and burrs resemble those of chestnuts, but are smaller. On young trees the bark is smooth, and on older trees, it is broken into reddish-brown ridges.

The twigs and branches from young trees are useful for making the plant stands and garden tool carrier.

Where Golden Chinkapin Trees Grow

Golden chinkapins cluster along the western coast of North America from northern California to southern Oregon along the edges of pine and hemlock stands.

HAZEL

Small trees or shrubs, hazel reaches heights of three to six ft. Its leaves are hairy, oval, or elliptical, and have a heart-shaped base and coarse, double-toothed margins. In the spring, the hazel's staminate catkins resemble those of birch, but its buds are oval and its fruit is a tiny nut enclosed by a leafy husk. In autumn, the leaves of the American hazel turn dull yellow, while the leaves of the beaked hazel (hazelnut) become bright yellow. Hazel twigs are dark brown, ranging from smooth on American hazel to rough on beaked hazel.

Hazel shoots are strong and its bark—which ranges from reddish-brown to yellowish-brown—is often densely hairy, lending a unique velvet appearance to twig projects. Supple young branches are useful for building trellises.

Where Hazel Trees Grow

American hazel occurs from Maine and Ontario south to Florida and Kansas. The beaked hazel tree grows from Nova Scotia to British Columbia, south to Georgia and Tennessee, and west from Kansas to Oregon. It grows in thickets, in moist or dry conditions and light soil, at the edge of woods or beside walls.

WITCH HAZEL

Witch hazel can be identified by its odd yellow flowers, which consist of four twisting petals, each about three-quarters of an inch long. The flowers appear in autumn and continue to hang on the bare branches after the leaves have fallen.

Witch hazel is most often used for small projects, such as the trellis planter.

Where Witch Hazel Trees Grow

Witch hazel is a small tree or shrub that grows in shady ground, and in the undergrowth of forests throughout the eastern half of the United States and Canada and as far south as Texas.

HICKORY

Hickory has often been called the most durable of native American hardwoods. In fact, when twig furniture manufacturing became a commercial venture in 1899, the Old Hickory Furniture Company chose hickory as its sole wood, and even today continues to manufacture hickory furniture in the traditional manner. Hickory is most commonly used for joined furniture (with a mortise and tenon structure) as opposed to my nailed-together designs, which are much easier for the novice.

Hickory bark is usually smooth and grey when young, becoming irregular with age. Its frayed edges give it a shaggy appearance. There are 11 hickories native to North America that can be used for twig furniture. The shagbark hickory has a distinctive, shaggy bark composed of thin, narrow scales that curve outward at the ends. Shellbark hickory resembles shagbark, but its leaves are very long, from 15 to 20 inches. Mockernut hickory has fragrant leaves that are 8 to 13 inches long, with hairy stalks and narrow leaflets. Pignut hickory has a scaly bark that forms diamond-shaped ridges on mature trees, while bitternut hickory is distinguished from pignut by its smooth, grey bark. Water hickory produces leaves with reddish, hairy stems. Black hickory is easily recognizable because of its deeply furrowed black bark and its dark, reddish-brown nut. Nutmeg hickory's bark is scaly and reddish-brown, and its dark green leaves are often silvery-white on their lower surfaces.

Hickory saplings can be grown in a coppice, which is a woodland planted to yield a continuous harvest of twigs. Supple young branches are useful for trellis work, while larger pieces work nicely for chairs and shelves.

Where Hickory Trees Grow

Shagbark, shellbark, and black hickories grow on low hillsides and river bottoms, while pignut, mockernut, bitternut, and nutmeg grow in dry highlands. Water hickory is found along river swamps from southeastern Virginia to Florida and west to Texas. Most hickories grow throughout eastern and central North America.

CALIFORNIA LAUREL (OREGON MYRTLE)

California laurel has leaves that resemble the eastern mountain laurel, but they are broader ovals and smell like bay rum. It has a greenish-brown bark, either smooth or scaly, and is most often considered a shrub rather than a tree. California laurel is very hard when dry, and so is superb for building sturdy furniture.

Where California Laurel Trees Grow
California laurel grows along the extreme west coast in Oregon and California.

MADRONE (ARBUTUS)

This branch of the heath family is made up of more than 1,500 species growing in acid soils. Most are shrubs, and all have simple and—in most varieties—alternating leaves. Blueberries, rhododendrons, and heathers are familiar varieties of the heath family. Madrone can be easily recognized because of its thin, red-brown bark. Its wood is soft, and becomes hard and brittle when dry. Limbs two inches in diameter are useful for making chairs and tables, but smaller twigs should be soaked in a bucket of water and stored in a cool place until they are ready for use (usually within a week). Madrone's terra-cotta colored bark is particularly beautiful, and useful for trellises, the topiary standard, and the picture frame shelf.

Where Madrone Trees Grow
The Pacific madrone grows along the northwestern coast, from British Columbia as far south as San Diego, California. Texas and Arizona madrone trees grow in their respective regions, and are quite similar in appearance to the northern ones. Sourwood is a variety that occurs in Louisiana, Georgia, Tennessee, and the Carolinas. Lyonia grows throughout Florida and has a reddish-brown, usually scaly, bark that forms ridges on a twisted trunk.

MULBERRY

Mulberry belongs to a family that includes osage orange, commonly used for making archery bows. Two herbs, hop and hemp, are also included in the mulberry family. The three species most commonly used for building rustic furniture are red mulberry, Texas mulberry, and osage orange. Red mulberry produces deciduous leaves that are three to five inches long and two to three inches wide. It grows to heights of 60 ft., and its leaves turn yellow in the fall. Texas mulberry is similar but smaller, growing to only 15 ft. in height. Its leaves are usually only an inch long. Osage orange produces multi-veined, deciduous leaves between three and five inches long, which turn bright yellow in autumn. Often used for hedge plantings, osage orange is distinctive because of its thorny twigs.

Mulberry twigs are useful for many projects, such as trellises, fences, chairs, and plant stands. Close-grained osage orange is hard and strong, and once its thorns are clipped, it is useful for almost all rustic projects.

Where Mulberry Trees Grow

Red mulberry grows in rich woodlands throughout Ontario, New York, and Vermont, from Minnesota to South Dakota, and from Florida to Texas. Texas mulberry, as its name implies, occurs as a small tree or shrub throughout the state and in the arid southwestern areas of North America. Osage orange can be found throughout most of the south and central portions of North America. It can be easily identified by its greenish-yellow bark and rough, inedible fruit, which ranges from three to five inches in diameter.

PACIFIC DOGWOOD

The leaves of Pacific dogwood resemble those of flowering dogwood but are larger, about four to six inches long and two to three inches wide. Its bark ranges from dark brown to black and is usually smooth, with scaly plates clustered around the bases of large trees. Pacific dogwood's showy white petals usually number six instead of the four found on the eastern dogwood.

Twigs and branches of Pacific dogwood can be substituted for beech or any other eastern hardwood.

Where Pacific Dogwood Trees Grow

Pacific dogwood grows at low elevations in shaded, coastal areas of western North America from British Columbia to San Francisco.

SWEETGUM

In the summer, sweetgum can be identified by its five-lobed, star-shaped, aromatic leaves. During autumn, these bright green leaves turn a brilliant red and gold. Its fruit is easily recognizable by its long stem and woody, burl-like head about one-and-a-half inches in diameter. The sweetgum's bark is scored with grey to brown ridges.

Where Sweetgum Trees Grow

Sweetgum grows in wet soils from southwestern Connecticut and southern New York to southern Missouri and eastern Texas. It is found as far south as central Florida.

Last but not least, willow is the most important wood for making rustic twig furniture. Luckily, the tree (shrub) grows throughout most of North America, and there are more than 100 rapidly growing species in the northern hemisphere. Because willow hybridizes in nature, true identification is often impossible, but it is also not necessary for our purposes.

WILLOW

All willows have long, thin leaves that are slightly notched, and catkins with varying amounts of silky fuzz. Early spring pussy willows can be found along frozen rivers in many areas, where a few branches may be gathered and brought into a warm house to "force" the sight of spring. Pussy willows can also be found standing in bunches at city florist shops at a time when the snow has become a grimy March blanket. (Purchased willows can often be used for small projects such as miniature chairs.)

All willow is pliable when green, and its flexible twigs create the warped, sculpted style of most rustic twig furniture. Its strength and flexibility are invaluable for scallop edging and wattle fencing. Most rustic craftspeople rely on willow for arbors and trellises where bending is required. Willow has a long history—the North American Indians used young willow shoots to fashion baskets, fish traps, and cradle carriers. Willow shoots usually remain flexible for up to two weeks after harvesting, but it is a good idea to soak the shoots in a bucket of water in a cool place until you are ready to use them. Permit yourself a few tries at bending them before beginning your project.

Do not rush the bending and arching—slow and steady is the key here. With a little practice the novice can soon become an expert.

Where Willow Trees Grow

Willow usually grows along streams and creek beds, and in places where the soil is moist. Because most types of willow are similar, it is not necessary to identify each species. However, for those of you out on a willow-hunt in various parts of the country, I would like to mention some of the North American willows. In the western portions of the United States there are the Pacific willow, feltleaf willow, scouler willow, and hooker willow. The peachleaf willow grows throughout the south-central portion of the United States, as do the sandbar willow and the yewleaf willow. Balsam willow, bog willow, sage willow, and pussy willow are the most common willows of eastern North America. Diamond willow and hoary willow grow throughout most of North America in bogs and lowlands. Some of the finest willow in the world comes from areas where long growing seasons, cool nights, sunny days, and rich damp soil create ideal growing conditions for long straight shoots.

Willow roots easily, and is often planted in coppices. The most common fast-growing tree, willow provides shoots during its first year that are excellent for making baskets, and a full twig crop suitable for making furniture during its third and fourth year. To plant willow for future harvesting, cut 12-inch lengths of willow shoots and plant them 10 inches deep, 18 inches apart in rich soil, preferably along a creek bed. In three to four years, a good willow crop for making twig furniture will be ready to harvest. Willow requires pruning to permit young shoots to grow; it is nature's way of recycling!

Peeled Willow

While bark is left on for almost all twig pieces, some craftspeople are experimenting with peeled willow work. It is usually best to peel the willow in the spring and summer months when the trees are growing and the cells beneath the bark are dividing rapidly. Cut the willow poles before peeling. Using a sharp knife, score a line down the length of the pole through the bark, and the "skin" should slip off. If not, carefully pry the bark loose with your fingers. Smooth, barkless willow, the color of a Kansas wheat field, has the look of natural wicker.

CHAPTER 2

Basic Methods for Working with Twigs

THE FIRST REQUIREMENT, of course, is wood. Chapter 1, Finding the Wood, will tell you how to locate raw materials in your area. Try to find branches with interesting markings and unusual shapes, as they will help inspire your imagination and add uniqueness to your finished work.

Although most books on the subject suggest that wood should be cut in the winter to preserve the bark, I have not found this to be true, and have cut twigs in the spring and fall that have retained their bark as well. If, however, you want to strip the bark, cut in the summer when the trees are growing and the cells between the bark and the wood are dividing.

TOOLS AND EQUIPMENT

You will need the following tools and equipment to build your garden twig furniture:

A crosscut hand saw, coping saw, single bit axe, garden shears, and/or clippers will be necessary for gathering the twigs.

A ⅜-inch variable-speed drill (electric or cordless is best—using an old-fashioned hand drill will take a little longer to finish your project) with a selection of bits; a hammer; and galvanized flathead nails in #4p, #6p, #8p, #10p, #12p, and #16p sizes are required to assemble the pieces of your project. You will also need a marking pencil, measuring tape or ruler, safety glasses, and work gloves. (Always use safety glasses or goggles when working with wood to shield your face and eyes from flying wood chips and sawdust.)

Optional Tools and Supplies

You may also need some of the following:

- For finer projects, ¾-inch finishing nails.
- A crosscut saw or key-hole saw.
- A cordless drill or hand drill for working on location.
- A ⅜-inch reversible drill if available.
- A drift punch (10 to 12 inches long) or a pocket knife for some projects.
- A 12-gauge wire and a wood chisel, and a two-inch rubber mallet.
- Linseed oil and turpentine or polyurethane if a piece is to be used out-of-doors for prolonged periods of time. A spray bottle or electric airless sprayer for applying the linseed oil/turpentine mixture.

Workbench

There are probably as many different types of workbenches, or work stations, as there are woodworkers. The simplest benches (and often the best) are heavy planks of wood standing on four legs. The legs are usually connected by rails that help to brace them, and perhaps support a few shelves. Dried 2' × 4' hardwood boards can be glued, or nailed together to create a suitable width for your work area. Attach this top with nails, or nuts and bolts to 4' × 4's for the legs. Location and area help to determine the size of your workbench, as well as your personal woodworking style. It depends on what is comfortable for you. I have seen workbenches in a variety of widths, lengths, and heights. While some craftspeople choose to stand at a waist-high bench, others enjoy working on a knee-high version, where they are able to straddle the bench.

Many rustic furniture builders like to work outdoors, and don't have any use for a conventional workbench. Very often just a standing log is all that is required to help support a work-in-progress. One woodworker I know uses the open back of an old jeep as a work table, and moves his wood supply indoors to a heated basement to work on an old butcher block when the weather turns too cold. Rustic furniture can be built at the finest store-bought bench, but more importantly and in keeping with the spirit of the material, it can be built in the woods, in the garage, or at the kitchen table.

CHOOSING AND STORING BRANCHES

Always gather more branches than are required. Some of the lengths, diameters, and shapes you choose in the woods will not be suitable for the particular piece you are planning to build. It is a good idea to have a supply on hand.

Always gather more willow or other pliable branches than you need. It is not unusual to break a few during bending, especially when you are first getting started.

After each piece is cut, identify the part with a small slip of paper taped to the branch. This will help you quickly identify each branch as you assemble the project.

Fresh, green branches are suitable for all projects. Seasoned (dry) branches are suitable when bending is not required, especially for making chair and table legs. Only green branches can be used for the bendable parts. For best results, use fresh willow or vines within a few days of cutting. If this is not possible, stand the willow twigs in a bucket of water, placed where they cannot freeze. They can last for several weeks if you remember to keep the bucket filled with water. In order to keep vines supple, coil them into a wreath shape and submerge in a bucket of water with rocks placed on top of them to weigh the coil down.

BUILDING THE PROJECT

After the wood has been gathered and the pieces selected and cut to size, assemble the basic frame structure, following the directions given. When the sub-assemblies are complete, it often helps to have someone hold the pieces upright while you connect the two sub-assemblies. The basic frame is then ready for the addition of the other pieces, such as arms, back, and seat. The bent willow is generally applied last. Here again it is a good idea to enlist an assistant to bend the willow (or alder) and hold it in place while you drill the pilot holes and nail the pieces together.

Checking for Strength and Safety

When your project is complete, check the stretchers, rails, and all other connecting beams for strength. This is especially important for chairs. Turn your finished piece over, and try to move the connecting members to ensure that the joints are secure. The joints should not wobble or move. At this point, if there is play in the joints, you may have to add extra nails, being sure to drill pilot holes first.

About Nails

Flathead galvanized nails are used for most of the joinery. Their subtle grey coloring blends in nicely with most wood tones, while their broad, flat heads ensure a firm joint. Galvanized nails do not rust and their rough surfaces hold well in both green and seasoned wood.

Finishing nails with small heads (sometimes called panel nails) are used for attaching thin twigs, usually the decorative elements.

Nails are sized in terms of pennies (#p), originally signifying the price per hundred. A #2p nail is one inch long, a #4p is one-and-a-half inches long, a #6p is two inches long, and so on.

Keep an assortment of galvanized nails near your work area. When you select a nail for each joint, make sure that it is just a little shorter than the combined thickness of the two twigs you are joining. The drill bit you use should be slightly smaller in diameter than the nail you plan to use. Drill each hole to a depth that is three-quarters of the length of the nail. You want the nail to bite firmly into the second member of the joint.

Use branches as braces for strength and rigidity. Add the braces front-to-back and side-to-side to keep the piece from swaying. They should form a triangle with two of the perpendicular branches of the piece—for example, leg and cross beams, or leg and side rails. When selecting branches for braces, remember that forked pieces are decorative while still being functional.

After the piece is completely assembled, it is a good practice to inspect all the joints and add nails where necessary to strengthen the assembly. An additional nail is usually required where a beam, a rail, and a leg meet, so that three nails are used at the joint.

Pilot Holes

Drilling holes (called pilot holes) before nailing will keep the wood from splitting as it dries. Select a drill bit that is slightly smaller in diameter than the thickness of the nail you are using. Pilot holes should be snug and not as deep as the nail is long.

Butt Construction

When project directions call for butt construction, it simply means that the end of one member fits flush against the other to form the joint.

BARK AND VINE PROJECTS

Although each type of natural material has its own unique uses, to my way of thinking nothing is as versatile as tree bark. Throughout history, bark has been put to use in a variety of ways. Birch bark is the most commonly used, as its natural waxes make it waterproof. It is also very durable and remains in the soil after the tree's inner wood has rotted away. Many cultures have developed uses for bark. Native Americans used the tough bark of the white paper birch to cover the twig frames of their wigwams, and fastened large sheets of it over wooden frames to make canoes. They also made birch bark containers and, throughout the late 1800s and into the twentieth century, created birch bark souvenirs for the tourist trade. The Laplanders use bark to make plates and circular boxes, as well as for roofing shingles. In Switzerland, a large musical instrument called an alphorn, up to 15 ft. long, is made out of birch bark.

My first bark basket was an antique one that I bought in Northern Canada about 20 years ago. The vendor told me it was made by a Cree Indian in the 1800s. Its sturdy shape fascinated me, and I still marvel at its simple charm. The bark of the birch is reversed, so that the paper white is on the inside and the reddish hue of the inner bark is displayed on the outside. The bottom and the side closing are laced together with willow, and it has a bent willow handle. This basket has delighted me throughout the years, and has served to hold fresh or dried flowers (with a glass jar inside), French bread at a buffet dinner, and a heap of pine cones and red ribbons during the holidays.

My second experience with bark took place in North Carolina, where I discovered an Appalachian berry basket. This unique basket is folded from one piece of bark, and its cylindrical shape and the concave eye-shaped base are its distinctive features. I have seen similar baskets made by the Cherokee, and assume that the early mountaineers learned from them how to make this basket.

WORKING WITH BIRCH BARK

Bark taken from freshly cut trees is usually pliable enough to use within a day or two. If, however, you have to wait several days before you begin your project, it is a good idea to soak the bark in water. A walk through the woods will often lead you to pieces of naturally peeled bark that you can use for some of the projects.

BARK WOODS

Paper white birch, black birch, cedar, chestnut, box elder, eucalyptus, hickory, palm, tulip poplar (yellow poplar), white walnut, yew, mountain magnolia, ash, linden, and bass are all good barks to use for projects. Alder and fir might also be usable. It is a good idea to experiment with bark from local trees to see which are appropriate for projects.

PEELING THE BARK

Use only bark from recently fallen trees. Do not peel bark from living trees. Stripping the bark from live trees will cause the tree to die.

To peel the bark from the branch, score a deep line lengthwise through the bark with a sharp knife. Make two cuts around the branch, marking the section of the bark to be removed. Place the top of a chisel along the scored line and gently tap it with a mallet. Continue until the section of bark is removed. If the project requires pressed bark, press the bark between heavy books or large flat rocks or bricks until ready to use. Depending on where you are comfortable working, pressing the bark can be done indoors or outdoors. Although I have successfully peeled bark during all seasons, it is easiest in the summer when the sap is up.

VINES
Those pesky bramble vines that often infest suburban yards and smother trees and bushes in the wild are another fine source of material. There is an almost limitless supply growing along roadsides. In addition, pruning some of these vines enhances the surrounding countryside.

GOOD VINES FOR PROJECTS
Bittersweet, Boston ivy, clematis, grapevine, honeysuckle, ivy kudzu, Virginia creeper, and wisteria (ivy and grape) are vines that are easy to use. Blackberry and raspberry are useful too, but must be dehorned.

CHAPTER 3

Fencing, Trellises, & Arbors

Wattle Border Fence

SKILL LEVEL: INTERMEDIATE (SHORT VERSION),
EXPERIENCED (TALL VERSION)

Yes, this fence made of saplings is a neat and attractive kind of rustic fence that looks well with almost any kind of planting.

THE JUNIOR GARDEN CLUB OF AMERICA,
BETTER HOMES & GARDENS, JULY 1933

THIS ARRANGEMENT of woven twigs is reminiscent of the fences devised by early settlers to separate their property and border their gardens. Wattle fences are fast becoming a versatile favorite of home gardeners, offering limitless possibilities by varying the rows of weaving. Three or four flexible shoots interlaced with slender twigs makes a charming natural edging for a low-growing herb garden, while the taller version can support a wall of sunflowers or climbing roses. A portable wattle fence adds instant drama and is a good backdrop for potted houseplants moved outdoors during warm weather.

TOOLS	
• Single bit axe for felling trees	• Crosscut hand saw
• Clippers or garden shears	• Ruler or measuring tape
• Marking pencil	• Sharp pocket knife
• Draw knife (optional)	• Drill and selection of bits (optional)
• Safety goggles	• Work gloves

MATERIALS

Willow, alder, mulberry, hickory, or any pliable branches are suitable. Choose sturdy branches for the posts and flexible saplings for weaving. The number of branches required depends on the size of the area you plan to enclose.

DIRECTIONS

The Edging

You will need straight branches 1 ft. long, with ¾" to 1¼" diameters for the posts, and ½" diameter pliable saplings, as long as possible, for the weaving. It is best to arrange the branches and build the edging in the garden near where the finished fence will stand. You will need approximately one branch for each 8" to 10" of fence.

1. Using a sharp pocket knife, sharpen the ends of the posts. In soft ground, the posts can be hammered directly into the earth with the aid of a wooden mallet, or dig post holes spaced 8" to 12" apart with a sharp garden trowel. Install an *uneven* number of posts, or when you reach the end of the first row, you will have to go in front of or behind two neighboring posts.

2. The edging uses the basic weaving technique of "under and over"; however, because you are working with upright posts you are actually weaving in front of one and behind the next. Working from the top of the installed posts, gently bend flexible sapling in front of one post and behind the next post.

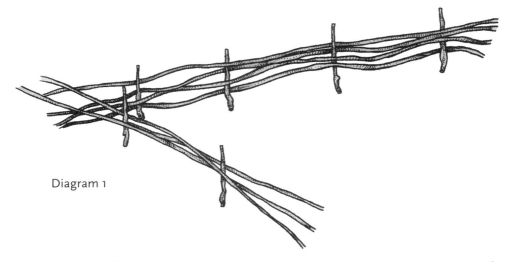

Diagram 1

Three to five rows of wattle weaving provides an attractive edging for ground-hugging plants.

The Border Fence
You will need straight branches 4 ft. to 6 ft. long, with 1" to 1½" diameters for the posts, and ½" to 1" diameter flexible branches, as long as possible, for the weaving. While it is easier to install the posts and do the weaving on site, it is possible to construct this version in the workshop and install it after it is complete. For on-site construction, the number of posts required depends on the area you plan to fence. A workable workshop size is 3 ft. wide and 4 ft. to 5 ft. high.

Sharpen the post ends with a sharp pocket knife or a draw knife. If you are working on-site, hammer an uneven number of posts directly into the earth, 10" to 15" apart, with the aid of a wooden mallet or maul. Continue with the weaving technique described in step 2 (edging procedure).

Portable Wattle Fence

This interpretation places the branch posts in a split log base. You will need a log with a diameter of 6" to 8", 5 ft. to 8 ft. long. If you don't have access to logs of this dimension, contact a saw mill, and have one split in half at the mill. With the split side down, use a drill and bit to drill holes large enough to fit the upright post branches snugly. Drill holes approximately 1 ft. apart. Refer to the diagram and place the upright branch posts in the base of the split log. Repeat the edging directions, above, for wattle weaving.

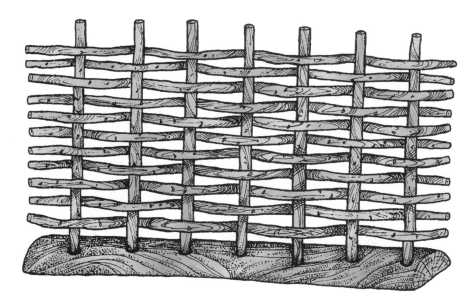

Diagram 2

Scallop Edging

The loveliest flowers the closest cling to earth.

JOHN KEBLE

THIS SIMPLE edging fence is perfect for the herb or flower bed where low-growing blossoms like to trail and peek out through the horseshoe loops. It can be made in any length and its portable construction makes it handy to install along raised beds, or a garden path.

MATERIALS

Use woods such as willow, beech, cedar, hickory, or mulberry. You will need two straight poles, 82" long and 1½" to 2" in diameter for the rails; three straight poles, 7" long and 1" in diameter for the braces; and two straight poles, 18" long and ¾" in diameter. You will also need a selection of pliable

		DIAMETER	LENGTH	
NAME OF PART	QUANTITY	(INCHES)	(INCHES)	DESCRIPTION
Rails A	2	1½–2	82	straight/hardwood
Braces B	3	1	7	straight/hardwood
Stakes C	2	¾	18	straight/hardwood
Horseshoe arches D	6	¼–½	27	pliable

C U T T I N G   C H A R T

T O O L S

- Single bit axe for felling trees
- Garden shears or clippers
- Marking pencil
- Hammer
- Safety goggles

- Crosscut hand saw
- Ruler or measuring tape
- 1" variable-speed drill and selection of bits
- Sharp pocket knife
- Work gloves

branches, such as willow, alder, mulberry, or cedar for the horseshoe arches. Galvanized flathead nails in assorted sizes and 1" finishing nails will also be necessary.

Cutting the Branches

1. Cut two 1½" to 2" branches for the rails A, each 82" long.
2. Cut three 1" diameter branches for the braces B, each 7" long.
3. Cut two ¾" diameter branches for the stakes C, each 18" long.
4. Cut six ¼" to ½" diameter pliable branches for the horseshoe arches D, each approximately 27" long.

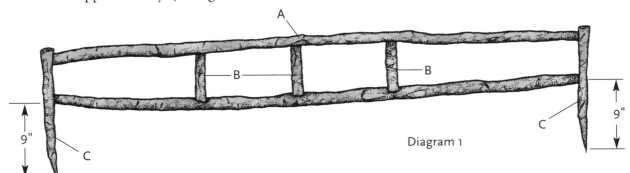

Diagram 1

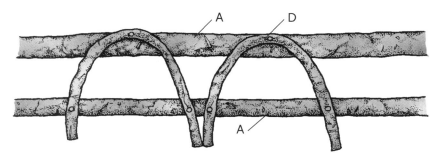

Diagram 2

Building the Basic Edging

1. Arrange the two rails A on the workbench. Using a pencil, mark the mid-point at the center of each rail (41"). The center brace will be attached to the rails at these marks.
2. Mark two points at 15" right and 15" left of the mid-points on both rails.
3. Butt the center brace B, between the two rails A at the mid-point mark. Drill a pilot hole through rail A into B from the top, and nail in place. Turn the construction over and drill another pilot hole. Nail through the second rail A into B as before until all three braces are nailed to the top and bottom rails.
4. Continue and fasten the other two braces B to the right and left of center as marked.

Adding the Stakes

Butt one stake C against both rails, allowing 9" to extend past the bottom rail. This sharpened end is inserted in the ground. Drill pilot holes and nail stake C in place into the ends of the top and bottom rails. Repeat this for the stake C at the other end of the rails.

Adding the Horseshoe Trim

1. Carefully bend one horseshoe twig D. Refer to diagram 2 and arrange one end of D against the bottom rail A. Drill and nail D in place where it meets the bottom rail; arching it along the top rail A, drill D and nail it to the top rail. Bring it down and nail it to the bottom rail with a pilot hole through D.
2. Repeat with the remaining horseshoe arches.

Farm Fence

When I was a boy, they built that fence of ancient trees,
over there where the wheat lot meets the sky.

EDWARD BENJAMIN

THIS SIMPLE FENCE made of cedar poles is as at home in the suburbs as it is on the farm. To calculate the amount of wood you will need, mark off the fence line with stakes, allowing 8 ft. to 10 ft. intervals between the posts. The twin posts are connected with two 6" stretchers that also serve to hold the stringers.

MATERIALS

Choose straight poles 3" to 5" in diameter and at least 8 ft. long for the posts. The stringers should be 3" to 4" in diameter and at least 10 ft. long. NOTE: The fence posts shown here stand 4½ ft. above the ground, and are set 2 ft. into

31

TOOLS	
• Single bit axe for felling trees	• Chain saw (optional)
• Crosscut hand saw	• Shovel
• Carpenter's measuring tape	• Marking pencil
• Clippers or garden shears for trimming small branches	• Clamshell-type post-hole digger (optional)
• Tamping iron (optional)	• ⅜" variable speed drill and bits
• Hammer level	• Chalk line (optional)
• Stakes	• Safety goggles
• Work gloves	

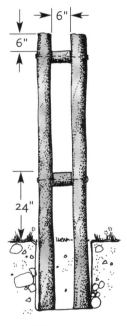

Diagram 1

the ground. The posts are spaced 10 ft. apart, and the stringers are 12 ft. long. If you place the posts at 8 ft. intervals, use 10 ft. stringers. Use pilot holes and rough-finished galvanized nails to connect the stretchers to the posts.

DIRECTIONS
Getting Started and Setting the Posts
1. Using a chalk line or pegs and string, mark off the area.
2. Mark off the locations for the posts at 8 ft. to 10 ft. intervals.
   NOTE: The length of the stringers helps to determine the post spacing. For example, if your stringers are 10 ft. long, the posts should be spaced at 8 ft. intervals.
3. Because the twin posts are only 6" apart, it is best to dig one long hole that can accommodate both posts. Using the shovel (or post-hole digger) dig a hole 2 ft. to 3 ft. deep and long enough to set the poles 6" apart (diagram 1).
4. Set the twin posts in the ground, and backfill with soil.

Connecting the Posts with Stretchers

1. Using the drawing as your guide, butt a stretcher between the twin posts, and use pilot holes and nails to join it to both posts 6" from their tops.
2. Butt another stretcher in place, and nail it to both posts 2 ft. from the bottom (diagram 1).
3. Use the tamping iron or shovel to press the soil firmly around the twin posts.
4. Continue assembling the fence by digging holes where indicated, setting the rest of the posts in place, adding the stretchers, and then backfilling the holes with soil and tamping the soil around the posts.
5. To turn a 90 degree corner in the fence, use three posts as shown in diagram 2.

Adding the Stringers

Lay the stringers across the stretchers as pictured. This fence design can be expanded as necessary.

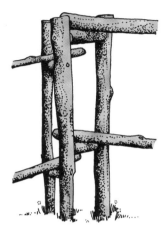

Diagram 2

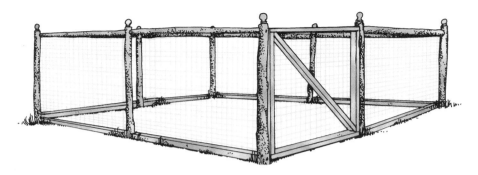

Garden Pen

The occupation is so delightful to me
as the culture of the earth…
and no culture comparable
to that of the garden…
But though an old man I am
but a young Gardner.

THOMAS JEFFERSON

A SUCCESSFUL HOME GARDEN should be fenced to discourage crowds of veggie- and blossom-feasting critters, who have been known to eat everything from asparagus to zinnias. This basic square enclosure, built with cedar poles and galvanized wire fencing, is an attractive way to protect your garden. Use creative decorative elements to reflect your own personal style. Wooden finials from a building supply center, and aluminum storm-door curves from a yard sale, all painted brilliant blue, enhance this garden setting. Use your imagination to create ornamentation. Whether you have an established garden or are starting a new one, the basic instructions can be adapted to your site.

TOOLS

- A single bit axe for felling trees, and/or a chain saw are required if you choose to cut your own cedar poles

- Clamshell-type post-hole digger (available at tool rental equipment locations)

• Crosscut hand saw	• Carpenter's measuring tape
• Marking pencil	• Tamping iron (optional)
• Shovel	• ⅜" variable-speed drill and drill bits
• Hammer	• Level
• Chalk line (optional)	• Wire clippers or tin snips
• Safety goggles	• Heavy-duty work gloves

MATERIALS

Nine straight 3" to 4" diameter cedar poles at least 7½ ft. long are required for the posts. Seven 1½" to 2" diameter cedar poles 8 ft. long (and one 4 ft. long) are used for the top rails. NOTE: Cedar poles can be purchased at lumber yards and home centers. Seven four-by-four cedar fence rails, 8 ft. long are required for the base rails. You will also need a 5 ft. × 64 ft. roll of medium-weight wire field fencing, sometimes called sheep fence; and a 3 ft. wide × 64 ft. long roll of chicken wire (both available at hardware stores or home and farm centers). NOTE: Sheep fencing has 2" × 4" openings, and will prevent large animals such as deer or dogs from getting into the garden. Chicken wire, with its smaller holes, will deter bunnies and rodents. Galvanized common nails are used to connect the posts to the top rails, and heavy-duty fence staples attach the wire fencing to the structure. The gate is constructed out of two-by-fours and hung on two gate hinges. Install a hook and eye or the latch of your choice.

DIRECTIONS

Getting Started and Setting the Posts

1. Using a chalk line or other pegs and string, mark off the area to be enclosed.

2. Mark off the locations for the posts at 8 ft. intervals, allowing for a 4 ft. wide gate opening. The decorative 4 ft. gate is wide enough to accommodate a wheelbarrow.

3. NOTE: Post holes should be 2½ ft. deep. Dig the holes for the posts, using the clamshell post-hole digger.

4. Place the first post in the hole and use a shovel to backfill the hole with dirt. Repeat with the remaining posts (diagram 1).

Adding the Top Rails and Base Rails

1. Using pilot holes, nail a top rail between two posts as shown in diagram 2.

2. Repeat with remaining top rails, taking into account the 4 ft. gate opening.

3. Using pilot holes, nail a four-by-four base rail between two posts as shown in diagram 3.

4. Repeat with the remaining base rails.

Diagram 1

Diagram 2

Diagram 3

Attaching the Wire Fencing

NOTE: The wire is stretched between the posts, and is stapled to the posts, and to the top and bottom rails.

1. Installing the wire will be easier if you have help. Stretch the wire sheep fencing between the posts, making sure to keep it taut. Staple it in place with heavy-duty fence staples. Continue keeping the wire taut, and attach it to the top and bottom rails with staples.

2. Install the chicken wire on the bottom rails and the posts, using the heavy-duty fence staples as in step 1 above.

The Gate

Construct the 4 ft. wide gate out of two-by-fours (diagram 4). Attach the sheep fence and the chicken wire to the gate in the same manner as above. Hang the gate with heavy-duty gate hinges.

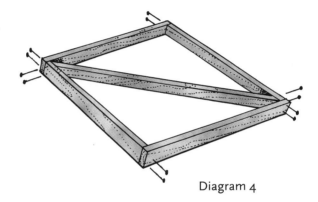

Diagram 4

The Garden Gate

*Sure she's the girl you used to swing
down by the garden gate.*

> DEAR OLD DONEGAL,
> A TRADITIONAL IRISH TUNE

IT TAKES MORE than flowers, herbs, and vegetables to establish a beautiful garden, and I can't think of anything more appropriate than the addition of the quintessential garden gate. Here is a rustic gate, perfect in almost any setting. It is designed to function as a swinging entry when installed between fence posts, but its whimsical twig lettering offers a decorative element and it is perfect anchored in the garden among the scented cowslips, parsley, and lemon balm.

CUTTING CHART

NAME OF PART	QUANTITY	DIAMETER (INCHES)	LENGTH (INCHES)	DESCRIPTION
Side supports A	2	1	42	hardwood
Stretchers B	2	1	29	hardwood
Top beam C	1	1	29	hardwood
Brace trims D, E & F	3	½–1	35–45	forked hardwood

TOOLS

• Single bit axe for felling trees	• Crosscut hand saw
• Clippers or garden shears	• Ruler or measuring tape
• Marking pencil	• Hammer
• Drill with a selection of bits	• Safety goggles
• Work gloves	

MATERIALS

Use any hardwood such as beech, birch, or willow. Lengths will range from 29" to 42" and with 1" diameters for the gate frame. Three forked branches (any hardwood), 35" to 42" long and ½" to 1" in diameter, will be needed for the brace trim. Use pliable shoots (willow or alder) for the lettering. You will also need galvanized flathead nails (#2p, #3p, #4p, #6p) for the gate and ¾" finishing nails or tacks for the letters.

DIRECTIONS

Cutting the Branches

1. Cut two 1" diameter branches for side supports A, each 42" long.
2. Cut two 1" diameter branches for the stretchers B, each 29" long.
3. Cut one 1" diameter branch for the top beam C, 29" long.
4. Cut three forked branches with diameters from ½" to 1", and lengths from 35" to 45" for the brace trim D.

Building the Gate

1. Begin construction from the bottom. Butt the bottom stretcher B between side supports A. Drill pilot holes and nail stretcher in place from the outside of A.
2. Add top stretcher B in the same manner.
3. Butt the side supports A against the top beam C, and with pilot holes, nail from the outside of C into the ends of side supports A.

Adding the Brace Trim

1. Lay the construction down on a flat surface. Lay the middle forked brace trim D on the top stretcher B. Butt the bottom single stem of the forked brace against the bottom stretcher B. Drill pilot holes through forked brace D, and both stretchers B. Nail in place using galvanized nails.

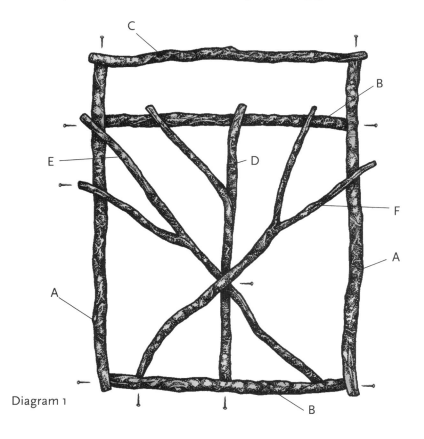

Diagram 1

2. Diagonally overlap brace trim E on the left side-support A, with the end butting against the bottom stretcher B. Nail to parts A and B with pilot holes.

3. Repeat with remaining brace trim F, and nail in place.

Adding the Lettering

The letters are formed with pliable twigs. The G is made up of five parts, nailed together using four thin finishing nails. It could also be made like the E which is formed by bending a supple twig into a U-shape and attaching the center line with a finishing nail. The same technique is used to form the A.

The R is made up of three parts, the D of two, and N is one supple twig with two bends.

Arrange the letters between the top stretcher B, and the top beam C, trying to keep them evenly spaced. Once satisfied with the placement, using thin finishing nails, nail the letters to the top stretcher and the top beam, B and C.

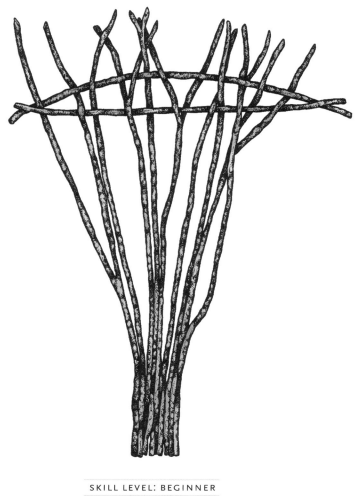

Willow Fan Trellis

April's air stirs in
Willow-leaves,
A butterfly
Floats and balances.

BASHŌ,
16TH CENTURY HAIKU

THIS SIMPLE FAN TRELLIS retains the traditional look of its lattice cousin, while encouraging all manner of climbers to grow along its spreading branches. Once you master this easy technique you will probably want to make it in various sizes for specific locations. Equally at home in town or country, the willow fan trellis makes a perfect window or porch screen, affording privacy while letting in light. Set in front of a wall or the side of a house, the trellis supports trailing vines, while helping to protect clapboards, ancient stones, or brick from invasive and sometimes damaging tendrils.

| | | DIAMETER | LENGTH | |
NAME OF PART	QUANTITY	(INCHES)	(INCHES)	DESCRIPTION
Uprights	11	¼–½	62	pliable
Horizontal weavers	2	½	45	pliable

C U T T I N G   C H A R T

T O O L S

- Single bit axe for felling trees
- Clippers or garden shears
- Marking pencil
- Hammer
- Work gloves

- Crosscut hand saw
- Ruler or measuring tape
- Drill with a selection of bits
- Safety goggles

MATERIALS

Use any pliable twigs such as willow, alder, or hazel, with the sturdiest ones for the uprights and the more flexible ones for the horizontal weavers. You will need eleven uprights 62" long, and ¼" to ½" in diameter. You will also need two horizontal weavers 45" long and ½" in diameter. An assortment of galvanized nails is required.

DIRECTIONS

Cutting the Branches

1. Cut eleven ¼" to ½" diameter branches for the uprights, each 62" long.
   NOTE: Try to include some forked branches as shown in the illustration.
2. Cut two ½" diameter branches for the horizontal weavers, each 45" long.

Assembling the Trellis

1. Place the middle three uprights together, side-by-side, on a work surface, making sure the ends are even.
2. Drill pilot holes partway through the three uprights, approximately 6" from the bottom, and nail in place as shown in diagram 1.

3. Nail two more uprights, one on either side of the three previously joined uprights, drilling pilot holes first (diagram 2). You now have five joined uprights.

4. Nail the remaining six uprights, three on either side, using pilot holes, as shown in diagram 3.

Fanning Out the Trellis

Interlace one horizontal weaver over and under the joined uprights at the top end, fanning the pliable verticals as you go. Repeat the weaving with the second horizontal twig continuing to gently fan the verticals. The force of the horizontal weavers should be enough to maintain the fan shape.

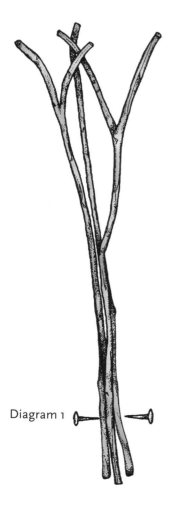

Diagram 1

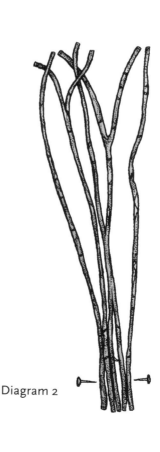

Diagram 2

Hints for training vines around the trellis:
Some vines may require a bit of help to encourage them to cling to the trellis uprights. Tie them loosely with soft twine or yarn so as not to damage the tender shoots.

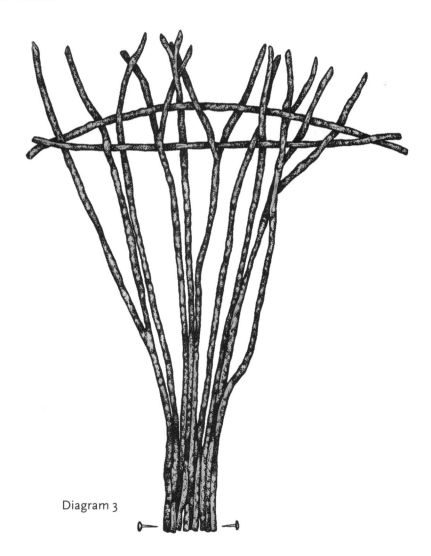

Diagram 3

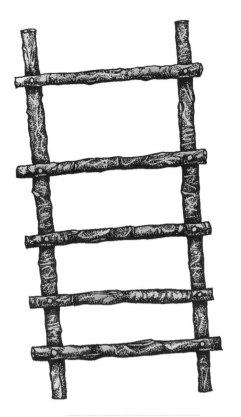

Simple Trellis & Trellis Arbor

SKILL LEVEL: BEGINNER

Here canopied reaches of dogwood and hazel,
Beech tree and redbud fine-laced in vines,
Fleet clapping rills by lush fern and basil…

ANNE SPENCER

IT IS EASY TO CREATE interesting garden architecture with this plain and natural design. One trellis is the perfect support for training climbing plants, deciduous or evergreen, annual or perennial. By the simple addition of two braces to three structures an arbor is created to help extend the landscape or serve as a garden centerpiece. For a dramatic departure from the usual flowering vines, try growing hops along these rustic branches for a distinctive autumn display of dainty golden cones.

46

NAME OF PART	QUANTITY	DIAMETER (INCHES)	LENGTH (INCHES)	DESCRIPTION
C U T T I N G C H A R T				
Side supports A	2	1½	80–90	straight
Overlap beams B	5	¾–1	26–36	straight

T O O L S

• Single bit axe for felling trees	• Crosscut hand saw
• Clippers or garden shears	• Ruler or measuring tape
• Marking pencil	• Drill with a selection of bits
• Hammer	• Safety goggles
• Work gloves	• Pocket knife (optional)

MATERIALS

Use wood like birch, cedar, hazel, maple, mulberry, or willow. To build one trellis you will need two 1½" diameter straight branches, 80" to 90" long; and five ¾" to 1" diameter branches, 26" to 36" long. Galvanized flathead nails in assorted sizes (#4p, #6p, and #8p) are used to join the pieces.

DIRECTIONS

1. Using a pencil and ruler, mark the points where the overlap beams B will be added to the side supports A to form the structure. Place the bottom beam approximately 10" up from the bottom of both legs. The top beam is placed approximately 12" down from the top of both legs. Each beam extends approximately 8" beyond the side supports. Adjust all measurements to suit your location.
2. Drill pilot holes through the overlap beams and partway through the side supports; nail in place using galvanized nails.

NOTE: To create the simple trellis arbor, build three trellises (as above) with identical dimensions. Rest one trellis on the top overlap beams of two vertical trellises to form the roof; nail in place with pilot holes. Angle two cross braces C along the inside planes, between the roof side supports and the standing side supports.

The arbor is simply three trellises—two trellises in their upright (vertical) position, joined by one horizontal trellis, placed on top as a roof, connected with two cross braces for stability.

A note on training vines:

Vines growing on arbors need to grow horizontally as well as vertically, and very often become extensions of their supports. A bit of training may be required, and you will want to be gentle with the young shoots. Sometimes all that is required is a simple arrangement, for the sticky tendrils soon take hold. For thicker branches, such as rose canes or grapevines, it is best to tie them loosely with soft twine.

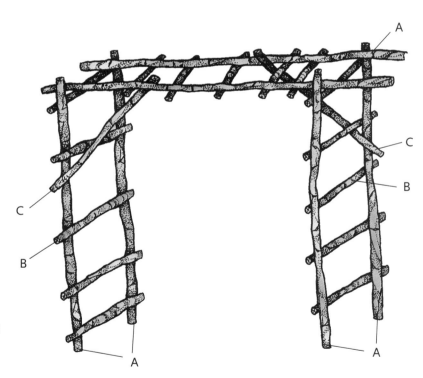

Diagram 1

Arched &
Vine=Wrapped
Arched Trellis

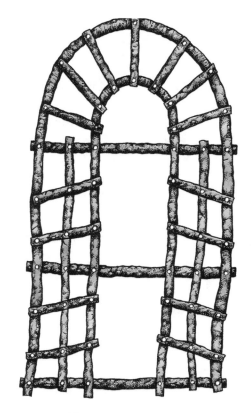

Rise; and put on your foliage, and be seene
To come forth like the Spring-time, fresh and greene.

ROBERT HERRICK

SKILL LEVEL: BEGINNER

MAKE AN ARCHED TRELLIS to help train trailing Rugosa roses for summer fragrance and you will be treated to an enchanting tangle of autumn rose hips. By altering the placement of two or three of these structures you will be able to add a dramatic dimension to your outdoor setting which promises year-round interest. Spring offers tender shoots, and summer lush and plentiful blossoms. Winter too has its special appeal in the garden when rabbits and birds feed on seed pods left attached to trellis branches.

49

	CUTTING CHART			
NAME OF PART	QUANTITY	DIAMETER (INCHES)	LENGTH (INCHES)	DESCRIPTION
Overlap beams A	3	1–1½	36	straight
Braces B	15	½–1	12	straight
Side supports C	2	¾	44	straight
Center arch D	1*	½–¾	124*	pliable
Basic arch E	1*	¾–1½	156*	pliable

*NOTE: These are the exact measurements, but it is unlikely that you will be able to locate one usable, pliable twig with this diameter and length. See options 1, 2, and 3 for additional construction techniques.

TOOLS	
• Single bit axe for felling trees	• Crosscut hand saw
• Clippers or garden shears	• Ruler or measuring tape
• Work gloves	• Drill with a selection of bits
• Hammer	• Safety goggles

MATERIALS

Use woods like birch, beech, cedar, hickory, or willow. Lengths should range from 9" to 80" and diameters from ½" to 1½". A selection of pliable branches, as long as possible, ½" to 1" in diameter, will be needed for the arched top. Gather an assortment of supple vines, such as grapevine, for the vine-wrapped arched trellis. Galvanized flathead nails in assorted sizes (#4p, #6p, and #8p) and finishing nails (¾") will also be required. The arched trellis is 3 ft. wide and 6 ft. high. Heavy gauge copper wire may be required for lashing short parts together.

DIRECTIONS

Cutting the Branches

1. Cut three 1" to 1½" diameter branches for overlap beams A, each 36" long.
2. Cut fifteen ½" to 1" diameter branches for the braces B, each 12" long.
3. Cut two ¾" diameter branches for the side supports C, each 44" long.

4. If possible, cut one ½" to ¾" diameter branch for the center arch D, 124" long; or cut two straight ¾" diameter branches 44" long, and one pliable ¾" diameter branch approximately 40" long.

5. If possible, cut one ¾" to 1½" diameter branch for the basic arch E, 156" long; or cut two straight ¾" diameter branches 60" long and one pliable ¾" diameter branch 64" long as shown in option 2; or cut two pliable branches, each approximately 82" long as shown in option 3.

Laying Out the Basic Framework

1. Construction begins with the basic arch, part E. With your gathered materials close at hand, decide on your construction technique.

2. NOTE: All beams A *overlap* across the basic arch E. (Option 1): The beams are spaced equally, approximately 22" apart from where the arch begins to curve. Drill pilot holes through the three overlap beams A and the basic arch E at the points where they join. Nail in place using galvanized nails.

3. (Option 2): In this model the basic arch is formed with three parts: two side supports C, and one center arch D. Drill pilot holes through the three overlap beams A and the basic arch E, at the points where they will join (see diagram). Nail in place using galvanized nails. Carefully bend a pliable ¾" diameter branch, approximately 40" long to form the top arched piece of E; join the ends of this arched piece to the sides of E by lashing them together with copper wire. NOTE: Copper wire weathers to a nice green patina and

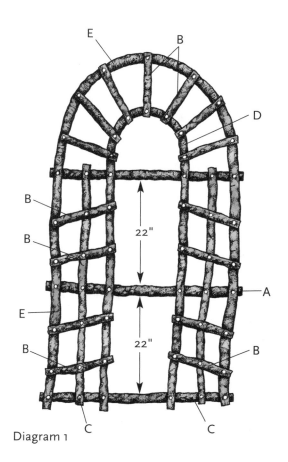

Diagram 1

blends in perfectly with outdoor rustic work. Add the remaining overlap beam to the construction, spaced approximately 2 ft. down from the arch.

4. (Option 3): In this example the basic arch E is formed with two separate branches, each approximately 82" long, which are lashed together, using copper wire, at the top. Add the three pre-drilled overlap beams, spaced approximately 22" apart as shown in the illustration.

Adding the Center Arch and Side Supports

1. The center arch is nailed to the three overlap beams using pilot holes in the same manner as the basic arch. Using one, two, or three branches, form the center arch and nail in place.

2. Center the side supports C between the basic arch E and the center arch

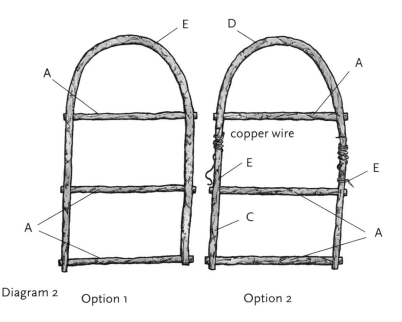

Diagram 2   Option 1   Option 2

D, and nail, from the back, to the overlap beams, with pilot holes and galvanized nails.

Adding the Braces

NOTE: The braces B are spaced approximately 8" apart from each other. Using pilot holes and two nails for each brace, nail each brace, from the front, to both arched members, the center arch D and the basic arch E. Follow the arched shape of the top, and the braces will form a fan-shape as they are installed.

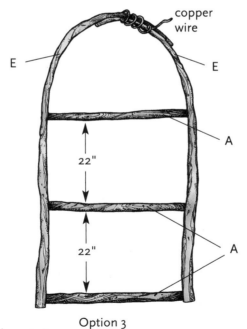

Option 3

Diagram 3

VINE-WRAPPED ARCHED TRELLIS

NAME OF PART	QUANTITY	DIAMETER (INCHES)	LENGTH (INCHES)	DESCRIPTION
Overlap beams A		same as arched trellis		
Braces B	8	½–1	12	straight
Side supports C		same as arched trellis		
Center arch D		same as arched trellis		
Basic arch E		same as arched trellis		

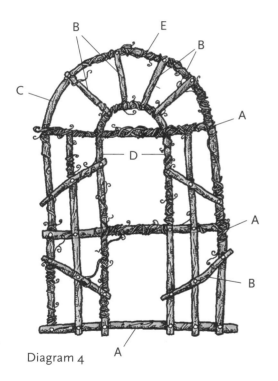

Diagram 4

DIRECTIONS

Follow the cutting directions for the Arched Trellis, but you will only cut eight branches, ½" to 1" in diameter, and 12" long for part B. You will also be required to cut enough ½" to 1½" diameter supple vine to wrap around the structure. Vines are easy to twist and wrap when they are fresh, and surprisingly strong when they dry. They are very good for keeping your trellis straight and plants like to cling on the natural curlicues and tendrils.

Follow the directions above for *Laying Out the Basic Framework* and *Adding the Center Arch and Side Supports*.

Adding the Braces and Wrapping the Vine

1. Nail four braces B, in a fan-pattern from the basic arch to the center arch using pilot holes and galvanized nails. Nail the remaining four braces B, diagonally from the basic arch to center arch, in the section between the overlap beams.

2. Interlace slender pliable vines over and under all parts; continue to weave and wrap the vines until you are satisfied with the arrangement.

Diagram 5 Pair of arched trellises

Diagram 6 Vine-wrapped trellis centered between two arched trellises

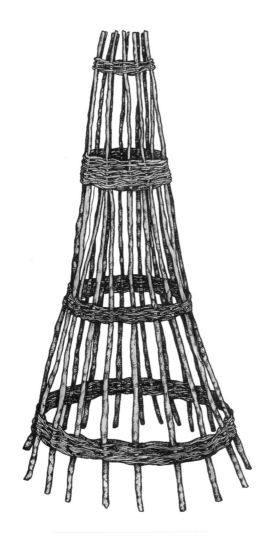

Cage Trellis

Habits and customs differ,
but all peoples
have the love of flowers in common.

CHINESE PROVERB

SKILL LEVEL: INTERMEDIATE

THE DENSE heart-shaped leaves of the exciting Moonflower (Ipomoea alba) and its giant trumpet flowers seem made for this 34" tall cone-shaped trellis. Its 17" diameter bottom easily fits over an 18" flowerpot or into a 24" pot. Well proportioned for the small terrace or deck, this moveable three dimensional trellis is just as practical indoors supporting a trailing plant.

T O O L S

- Garden shears or clippers
- Marking pencil
- Ruler or measuring tape
- Drill with a selection of bits
- Carpenter's compass

MATERIALS

You will need a piece of ¾" plywood 2 ft. square to make the pattern board to begin the weaving. The trellis requires twelve ¼" diameter pliable twigs, 34" long; and six ¼" diameter pliable twigs, 24" long. You will also need a selection of ⅛" to ¼" diameter supple branches (or vines) for the weaving. Use whatever branches and vines are available to you. The easiest branches to work with are long and supple, such as first year saplings and spring and fall vines. Local vine, such as grapevine, wisteria, or kudzu, may be used for the weaving. If you are using vines, gather them in the warm weather, and strip them of their leaves; weave the vines while they are still green (fresh). When they dry on the cage they will be very durable. If you must use winter vines, soak them in warm water to make them supple. Have 2 ft. to 3 ft. of string or wire handy to begin the weaving.

Diagram 1

DIRECTIONS

1. Place the plywood for the pattern board on a work table. Using the pencil and carpenter's compass center a 17" diameter circle on the board. Mark off eighteen points evenly spaced 3" apart. Drill eighteen ¼" diameter holes, at the marks, approximately ½" deep. These holes hold the twigs (spokes) in place during weaving (diagram 2).

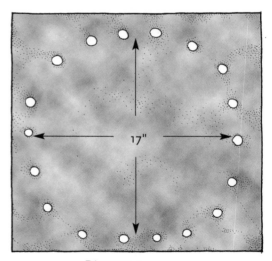

17"

Diagram 2

2. Arrange twelve 34" long spokes in every other pattern board hole. Gather the 12 spokes together at the top (see diagram 1), forming a 3" diameter, and loosely tie together with string or wire for a temporary hold. Begin weaving 2" from the top. Tuck one end of a twig or vine weaver behind one spoke and in front of the next, and continue over-and-under, in front of one spoke and behind the next until you have completed 6 or 7 rows. Tuck the ends of the weaver under and over itself to secure. The string may now be removed, or left in place until the project is completed.

3. Begin the second weaving section approximately 5" down the spokes from the last row of weaving. Continue weaving as above for 8 to 10 rows.

4. Now add the six remaining 2 ft. long spokes. Remove the construction from the pattern board. Insert one 2 ft. spoke next to a 34" installed spoke, pushing up into 4 or 5 rows of the weaving from step 3. Repeat with every 2 ft. spoke beside every other 34" spoke. Gently flare the 2 ft. spokes, and arrange all spokes in the 18 holes in the pattern board.

5. Begin the third weaving section approximately 8" down from step 3, this time weaving all 18 spokes. Weave 3 to 5 rows.

6. Begin the last weaving section approximately 9" down from step 5. Weave 4 to 6 rows. The trellis should remain standing in the pattern board until the green spokes and weavers dry, usually overnight.

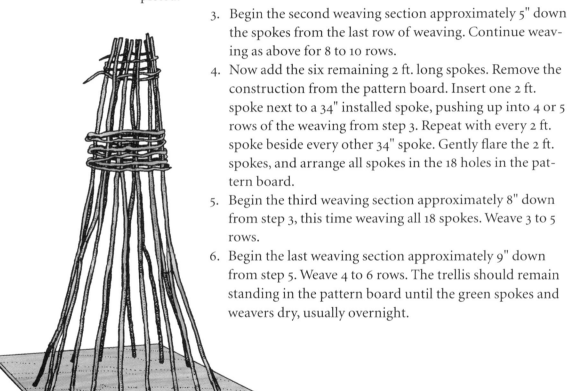

Diagram 3

Topiary
Standard

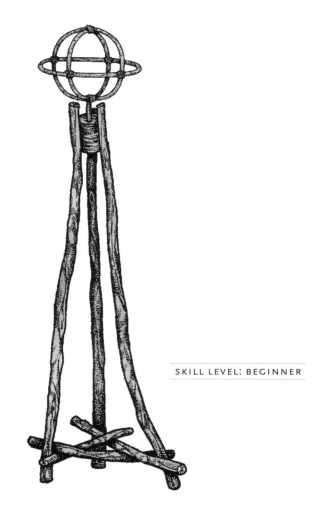

SKILL LEVEL: BEGINNER

Trailing odorous plants
which curtain out the day
with loveliest flowers

PERCY BYSSHE SHELLEY

CLIMBING TO THE TOP of any gardener's list would be this easy to construct topiary form. Its well proportioned size makes it adaptable to a wide variety of climbing vines. Ivies, clematis, morning glories, nasturtium, thunbergia, and sweet peas are just a few of the plants you will want to try on this dramatic standard. Clinging tendrils and winding leafstalks attach themselves to the sturdy uprights while twining greenery is trained on the willow sphere.

CUTTING CHART

NAME OF PART	QUANTITY	DIAMETER (INCHES)	LENGTH (INCHES)	DESCRIPTION
Legs A	3	¾–1	55	birch, willow, or any green hardwood
Spacer B	1	1	3½	hardwood
Stem support C	1	½–¾	4–8	willow
Stretchers D	3	½–¾	11–14	hardwood
Sphere	3	¼–½	26	pliable willow

TOOLS

• Single bit axe for felling trees	• Crosscut hand saw
• Garden shears or clippers	• Ruler or measuring tape
• Marking pencil	• Drill
• A selection of bits for Phillips-head drywall screws (1¼", 1¾", and 2")	
• Hammer and galvanized flathead nails (optional, to be used in place of screws)	
• Finishing nails	• Wire clippers
• Safety goggles	• Work gloves

MATERIALS

Any hardwood, such as birch, maple, or mulberry ranging from 45" to 55" long and 1" in diameter, is used for the basic structure. The legs splay outward, so be on the lookout for branches with interesting crooks and bends at one end. The willow sphere is made up of three supple willow twigs, ¼" to ½" in diameter and 26" long. You will also need one ½" diameter twig, 4" to 8" long for the stem support, and one 1" diameter branch 3½" long for the spacer, as well as a selection of ¾" diameter branches at least 11" long for the stretchers. Copper wire is used to bind the sphere.

DIRECTIONS

Cutting the Branches

1. Cut three ¾" to 1" diameter green (fresh) branches, each 55" long for the legs A.

NOTE: It is a good idea to use slightly tapered branches, with a bottom diameter slightly larger than the top diameter. These branches must be green and pliable in order to permit slight bending.

2. Cut one 1½" diameter hardwood branch, 3½" long for the spacer B.

3. Cut three branches ½" to ¾" in diameter and 11" to 14" long for the stretchers D.

4. Cut three supple willow twigs, each ¼" to ½" in diameter and 26" long for the sphere.

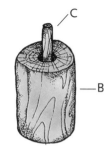

DIAGRAM 1   Spacer

Building the Topiary

1. Mark the center of the 1½" diameter spacer B. Drill a hole completely through the spacer at the center mark, wide enough to accommodate the stem support C, keeping a snug fit.

2. Fit the stem support C in the spacer-drilled hole. Add a dab of glue if needed (diagram 1).

Drilling the Pilot Holes and Adding the Legs

1. Check each of the three legs to be sure they will fit properly against the spacer. Use clippers to remove any interference.

2. Mark a point from the top of a leg A, 1½" down, and then a second point approximately 2" down from the first. Butt the leg securely against the spacer B, leaving 1" to extend beyond part B. Hold leg firmly in place and drill at the two premarked locations, through the leg and partway through the spacer.

3. Using a Phillips-head drywall screw (or galvanized nails), attach leg A to spacer B.

4. Repeat the above steps with the remaining two legs.

Adding the Stretchers

NOTE: If you have crooks and bends located at a point 8" to 12" from the bottom of the legs, you will want to attach the stretchers at this point. Permit the wood to dictate the

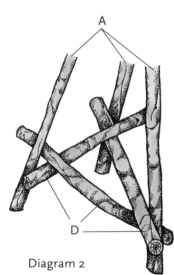

Diagram 2

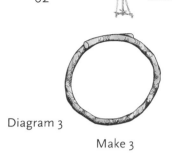

Diagram 3

Make 3

Diagram 4

Diagram 5

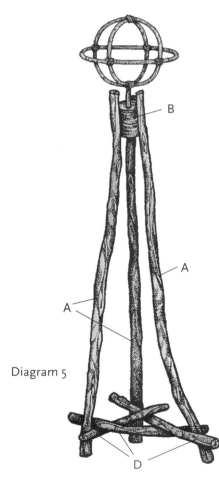

design. The stretchers D will be attached under and over each other, forming an equilateral triangle.

1. Drill a pilot hole approximately 1" to 1½" from the end of one stretcher D and through a point 8" to 12" up from the bottom of one leg. Using Phillips-head screws (or galvanized nails) attach the stretcher to the leg at this point.
2. Carefully extend the second leg outward; attach the stretcher to the extended leg in the same manner as the preceding step.
3. To attach the second stretcher D, place one end of the second stretcher over the installed stretcher, and using a pilot hole, attach to the same leg.
4. Attach the third stretcher over one installed stretcher and under the other.

Forming and Adding the Sphere

1. Form a ring with one of the 26" long pliable twigs, and secure the ends by wrapping them under and over each other as pictured (diagram 3).
2. Repeat the above step with the remaining two rings.
3. Fit the three pliable rings into the sphere, and join together at their meeting points with copper wire (diagram 4).
4. Attach the sphere to the installed stem support C with two or three finishing nails.
5. Stand the topiary stand upright, and check to see if it stands straight. Use a sharp knife or clippers, if necessary, to adjust the ends.

Window Box Trellis

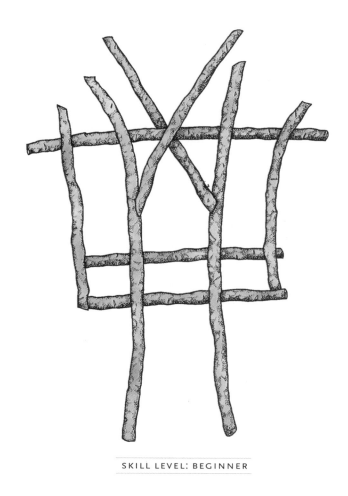

*More than anything
I must have flowers,
always, always.*

SKILL LEVEL: BEGINNER

DESIGNED WITH ORDER in mind, this mini trellis is well suited for window boxes with seasonal blooms. An evergreen ivy would be a good trainer along the trellis branches in most semi-protected window boxes. Allow the ivy to grow year round, and plant blue hyacinths, purple pansies, and yellow tulips for a springtime display. After blooming, replace the flowering bulbs with pink annuals such as geraniums or petunias for the summer, and then with fluffy mums in the fall, always keeping the trellised ivy as a background plant. Winter boxes may be filled with Irish juniper, white pine, or hemlock seedlings, sometimes found in the woods.

NAME OF PART	QUANTITY	DIAMETER (INCHES)	LENGTH (INCHES)	DESCRIPTION
Stakes A	2	½	20	pliable
Overlap beams B	2	½	12	straight
Side supports C	2	½	12	pliable
Cross braces D	2	½	12	straight
Top beam E	1	½	16	straight

C U T T I N G   C H A R T

T O O L S

• Hand saw	• Clippers or garden shears
• Ruler or measuring tape	• Marking pencil
• Drill (optional)	• Finishing nails
• Hammer	• Safety goggles
• Work gloves	• Pocket knife (optional)

MATERIALS

I used willow and mulberry for this project, but any hardwood would work nicely. It's easier to work with the branches when they are green, but you could alter the design a bit if only seasoned twigs are available. Lengths range from 12" to 21", with all diameters approximately ½". Finishing nails are used to join the parts, and if your twigs are green you can probably avoid drilling pilot holes.

DIRECTIONS

Cutting the Branches

1. Cut two ½" diameter pliable branches for the stakes A, each 20" long.
2. Cut two ½" diameter branches for the overlap beams B, each 12" long.
3. Cut two ½" diameter pliable branches for the side supports C, each 12" long.
4. Cut two ½" diameter branches for the cross braces D, each 12" long.
5. Cut one ½" diameter branch 16" long for the top beam E.

Assembling the Trellis

1. Place the two stakes A on a work surface and arrange them so that they are spaced approximately 7" apart. Mark a point 9" from the bottom of each stake A. Lay one overlap beam B across the stakes and nail it to stakes A where they cross.

2. Place the second overlap beam B across the stakes in the same manner at a spot approximately 4" apart from the attached overlap beam. Drill (if necessary) and nail to stakes A where they cross.

3. Place the side supports C under the overlap beams at the outside edges. Drill (if necessary) and nail in place.

4. Lay the top beam E over the stakes and the side supports at a location approximately 9" from the second overlap beam. Drill (if necessary) and nail the top beam to the stakes and to the side supports.

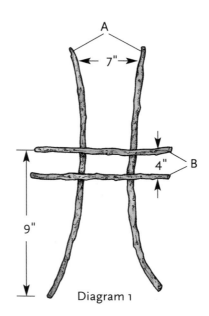

Diagram 1

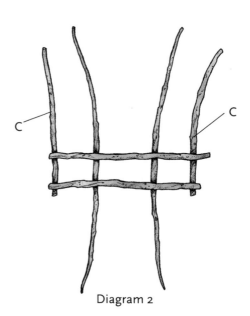

Diagram 2

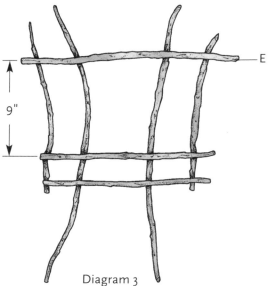

Diagram 3

5. Fit the cross braces D along the stakes so that they cross at the mid-point of the top beam, one under and one over, beveling the ends as needed. Nail in place (diagram 4).

Now that you have made the window box version, you may decide to try your hand at enlarging the design to build a full size trellis for the yard or porch screen.

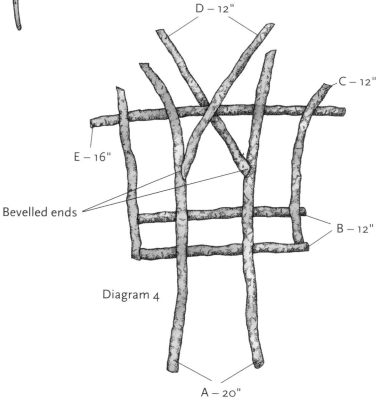

Diagram 4

Rustic Plant
Trainer

SKILL LEVEL: INTERMEDIATE

You are nearly as beautiful as the cascade
of roses that spills over the gatekeeper's tiny yard,
covers a gardener's cottage, or lattices the wall
of a country inn…

COLETTE

THIS HANDCRAFTED BRANCH rendition of the classic wire plant -
trateur (a frame for climbing vines) is sure to add individual style to your
garden or patio. The Rustic Plant Trainer, covered in meandering vines,
showcases both form and function. Perfectly suited for trailing ivy or clematis, the trainer will work equally well as a climbing pole for beans such as the
old-fashioned scarlet runner with its brilliant orange flowers. When winter
arrives this graceful shape will stand out against the snowy landscape, intro-
ducing a sculptural quality to enhance the view. This project can be put together in an afternoon.

67

T O O L S	
• Crosscut hand saw	• Garden shears or clippers
• Ruler or measuring tape	• Marking pencil
• Wire or string (optional)	• Safety goggles
• Work gloves	

MATERIALS

You will need eleven ¼" to ¾" diameter pliable twigs, 82" long for the stand, along with a selection of ⅛" to ¼" diameter supple vines for the connecting wreaths. A handful of finishing nails are used to attach several twigs to the wreaths. NOTE: The branches, as well as the vines, must be pliable in order to create the graceful shape of the trainer. Willow, dogwood, hickory, beech or birch are all good choices for the structure as well as grapevine, kudzu, or Virginia creeper vines.

DIRECTIONS

Wreaths and Vines

NOTE: The circumference of the top wreath is 62" and is composed of two pliable lengths of Virginia creeper. The circumference of the bottom wreath is 48" and uses one 100" length of ¼" diameter grapevine. The middle vine wrapping consists of a 75" length of ⅛" diameter grapevine.

1. To form the bottom wreath, carefully bend the length of the pliable vine into a circle, wrapping and twisting the two pliable ends over one another.

2. Make the top wreath, following the directions in step 1.

Adding the Twig Stand

NOTE: Be sure that your straight twigs are supple so you can get them to splay out as shown in the illustration (see picture).

1. Slip one straight twig through the bottom wreath. Continue to place the straight twigs, evenly spaced, through the wreath. Attach a few twigs to the wreath with finishing nails as needed. Securing some twigs to the

wreath will add strength and stability to the completed structure, but it is not necessary to use nails at each junction.

2. When all eleven twigs have been threaded through the bottom wreath, stand the construction upright. Make sure it is standing straight before adding the top wreath. Use clippers to trim the bottoms as necessary to ensure that the trainer stands up straight.

3. Place the top ends of the straight twigs through the top wreath in the same manner as you did in step 1 above, using finishing nails as required.

Wrapping the Middle

1. Weave the middle vine under and over the straight standing branches approximately 50" from the bottom of the structure. Pinch in the middle as you weave the vine. NOTE: You may decide to use wire or string to draw in the middle before you begin weaving.

2. Some vines may require help to start them trailing along the supports. By tying young shoots loosely to the supports with soft string you will encourage them to climb.

Shelter Arbor (Cabana)

Windyridge, let winds unnoticed whistle round your hill!
SIR JOHN BETJEMAN

TWO EIGHT-FOOT STRUCTURES are joined with a roof made of forked branches to create this handsome walled arbor, perfect for wisteria vines. It can be a screen, or with awning canvas panels, it becomes a sheltered nook. Add a bench for garden gazing or pondside viewing. The first step in designing your version is to decide where it will be located. The measurements given here seem to work well for individual sections. Two or more sections may be joined to fit your needs and the site. Make it portable or stationary, permanent or temporary.

CUTTING CHART

NAME OF PART	QUANTITY	DIAMETER (INCHES)	LENGTH (INCHES)	DESCRIPTION
Side post rails A	2	2	96	hardwood
Beams B	3	1½–2	60	hardwood
Braces C	3	1½	30	hardwood
Horseshoe trim	5–8	½–1	80–90	very flexible
Roof	5 or more	¾–1½	36 or longer	forked, hardwood

TOOLS

- Single bit axe for felling trees
- Crosscut hand saw
- Clippers or garden shears
- Ruler or measuring tape
- Marking pencil
- ¾" variable-speed drill
- Hammer
- Safety goggles
- Work gloves

MATERIALS

You will need 2" and 3" diameter hardwood branches, from 28" to 96" long. Pliable willow shoots ½" to 1" in diameter, and approximately 85" long, are required for the hoops and trim. Forked hardwood branches, at least 3 ft. long, are used for the roof. Galvanized flathead nails are used and some finishing nails may be required to attach thin willow shoots to the design.

DIRECTIONS

1. Butt the bottom beam B between the two side post rails A, approximately 5" from the bottom of the rails. Nail with pilot holes through the side of the post rail A, into the end of the bottom beam B.
2. Butt and join the second beam B in the same manner 30" up from the bottom beam B.
3. Butt and join the top beam B in the same manner, 5" to 12" down from the top of post rails A.
4. Butt the middle brace C at approximately 30" between the two lower

beams B. Nail with pilot holes drilled through the top of the upper beam and the bottom of the lower beam.

5. Evenly space, and butt the remaining braces between the beams and join as above.

6. Carefully bend and add horseshoe trim as pictured, or as desired. Very often the twigs have a mind of their own, and will dictate the design to you. Allow your imagination to run free when adding trims and loops and fanciful embellishments.

NOTE: The basic design may be adjusted, and another version spaces the two lower beams 20" apart, and calls for braces C to be 20" long.

To make the cabana, place two panels at right angles (more or less), and join together with roof parts.

To set up the cabana outdoors, tap stakes in the ground and nail to the side post rails to keep the structure steady.

I'm sure you can think of many spots to place an outdoor cabana: near the pool or the pond, by the hot tub, in the herb garden, in a sheltered area up on the hillside, or out in the field behind the pumpkin patch. Use your imagination to adjust the basic design to create fences, gates, gazebos, and arbors. This project can be reshaped, and its branches shortened or lengthened to suit your needs.

MATERIALS To Cover the Cabana

3 to 4 yards 54" wide water resistant canvas (or other suitable outdoor fabric, such as sun- and fade-resistant nylon) for the roof. 5½ yards 54" wide water resistant fabric for the sides. Grommet tool and grommets (available at sewing centers and hardware stores). 24 yards of rope (a clothesline works nicely).

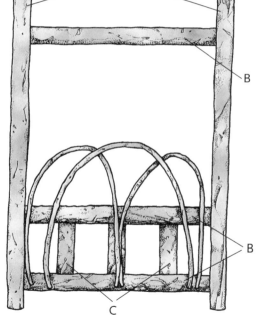

Diagram 1 Horseshoe trim

DIRECTIONS

Cut fabric pieces. NOTE: Fabric for the roof section will have to be sewn together. All fabric parts will need a 1½" hem along the edge. Measure the sections to be covered. Add ½" seam allowance around all the pieces that make up the roof section and the side panels, if needed.

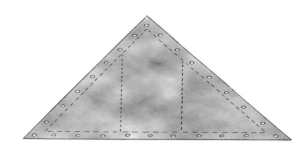

Diagram 2   Roof fabric panel

- Sewing and Hemming: Using ½" seam allowance, sew together the roof section. Sew a 1½" hem around the edge.
- Adding the Grommets: Attach the grommets with the grommet tool, spaced evenly approximately 6" apart, along the outside hemmed edge.
- Attaching the Fabric Roof: Using the rope, lace the roof section *inside* the cabana over and around the roof branches.
- Hemming the Two Side Panels: Sew a 1½" hem around all four sides of the side panels.
- Adding the Grommets: Attach the grommets with the grommet tool, spaced evenly approximately 6" apart along all four sides.
- Attaching the Side Panels: Using the rope, lace the side panels *outside* the cabana over and around the side post rails A.

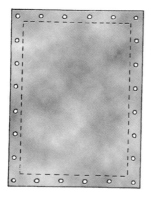

Diagram 3   Fabric side panel

Diagram 4   Lacing through the grommets

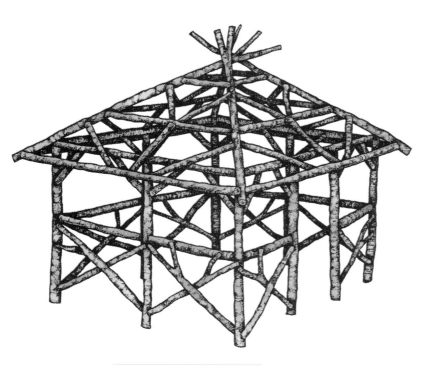

The Summer House

When covered with running vines,
the arbor becomes a canopy
under which a seat may be placed
in pleasant weather.

FRANK A. DE PUY, 1900

WHEN I BEGAN writing this book, a friend asked me to help him design an outdoor room that he could use as an arbor to provide support for some native grapevines that he discovered growing wild on his property. He wanted me to design a large project he would be able to construct by himself, hundreds of miles away from my home. At first it sounded like a difficult assignment, but the rough sketches soon developed into a design that he felt comfortable with, and he foraged, purchased, and collected timbers from various sources. Armed with some basic construction techniques, a good se-

T O O L S	
• Single bit axe for felling trees	• Chain saw (optional)
• Crosscut hand saw	• Clipper or garden shears
• Ruler	• Marking pencil
• ⅜" variable-speed drill and drill bits	• Hammer
• Sturdy step ladder	• Plumb bob
• Level	• Safety goggles
• Work gloves	

lection of 2" to 4" diameter straight branches, a small chain saw, a power drill, and with some willing assistants, my friend built his rustic structure. Chairs and a small log table were placed inside, and the gnarled and ancient grapevine shoots were planted along the supports.

My friend is delighted with his outdoor retreat. It is his special resting spot on lazy summer afternoons.

MATERIALS

The sides of the summer house are approximately 8 ft. tall and 10 ft. wide. Nine 8 ft. straight branches, with 4" diameters make up the basic structure; the doorway is 3 ft. wide. Eight 12 ft. straight branches with 3" to 4" diameters are required for the basic roof structure. Eight 3" diameter straight branches are used for the cross rails, and 2" diameter branches for the diagonal braces. Pilot holes and rough-finished galvanized nails are used to connect the posts to the top beam.

Stainless-steel nails will not rust and you may decide to splurge and use them for this project. Countersunk lag screws are used to attach diagonal braces. NOTE: To countersink lag screws drill a hole using a bit larger than the head of the screw. Countersink holes should be deeper than the depth of the head of the screw. When all screws are turned in, the holes may be plugged with pegs cut from branches (diagram 1).

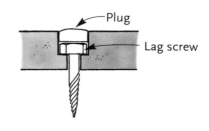

Diagram 1

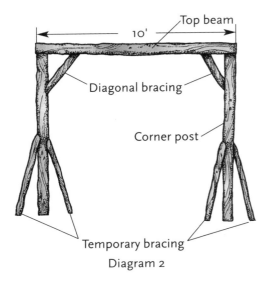

Top beam

10'

Diagonal bracing

Corner post

Temporary bracing

Diagram 2

Diagram 4   Center post

DIRECTIONS

1. It is important to begin with solid, straight poles for the posts to guarantee a straight and neat structure. Arrange each corner post plumb, at its desired location temporarily braced with two or three pieces of scrap lumber. These temporary braces hold the post in place while work begins on the structure (diagram 2).

2. Assemble the beams on top of the corner posts and join together with nails. Add one or two diagonal braces from post to top beam using a lag screw at each junction

Brace detail countersunk lag screw

Diagram 3

(diagram 3). These braces are permanent and help to strengthen the structure.

3. Plumb the center post on each of the three sides, and join to the top beam with nails. Add diagonal braces from center post to top beam using countersunk lag screws (diagram 4).

4. Arrange the two doorway posts in place, at approximately 3½ ft. from the corner posts, and attach to the top beam. Add diagonal braces (diagram 5).

   NOTE: The doorway opening is approximately 3 ft. wide and 8 ft. high.

5. Check that the posts are plumb, and join the rails to the posts at approximately 4 ft. from the bottom of the posts (diagram 6).

Diagram 5   Doorway

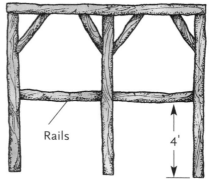

Rails

4'

Diagram 6

6. Add the cross braces to the sides (diagram 7). Forked branches work nicely here, for they add strength to the structure as well as interest. Remember, each rustic piece is an original.

7. If you have been working on your own until this step, help is usually required when adding the roof timbers. The heavy beams and braces will have to be handed to you. An extra pair of hands will be needed to raise and attach the hip rafters.

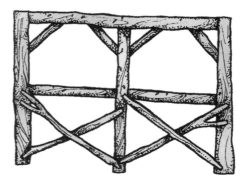

Diagram 7   Side section

Assemble the basic roof parts in place (diagram 8). Attach the roof beams to the hip rafters. Notice that the diagonal hip rafters extend and cross at the top. The roof beams extend approximately 12" beyond the corner posts to form the eaves (diagram 9). The roof will be filled in later with various braces (diagram 10).

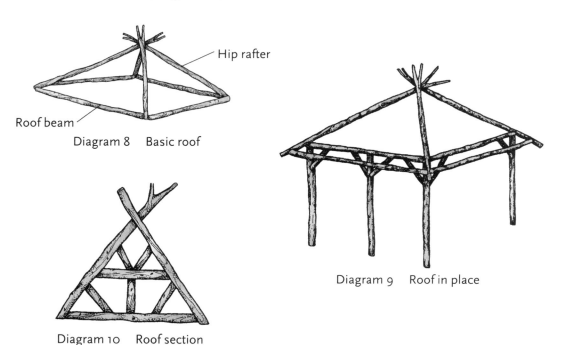

Hip rafter

Roof beam

Diagram 8   Basic roof

Diagram 10   Roof section

Diagram 9   Roof in place

8. Each roof section requires at least two additional beams, and five braces. Decorative curving branches are nice for braces.

Braces help to make your structure strong and straight. Add more braces, if needed.

NOTE: The Summer House shown in the photo section is a variation on the directions provided here. The Summer House in the photo has a shingled roof and a solid wood floor, both of which are beyond the scope of this book.

Remember that any of these projects can be changed or added to as long as you are comfortable with the basic design.

While grapevines are an excellent low-maintenance choice for most locations, The Summer House can support an almost endless array of handsome vine plants. Purple wisteria is an old favorite climber; it can be trained to twine around the poles and beams by wrapping young stems with soft twine. Eventually clusters of fragrant blue-violet flowers will bloom, creating a magical and sweet-smelling canopy.

Bittersweet, with its coiled and twisted stems, is an attractive climber in all seasons. It is at its best in the autumn when its summer green leaves turn a clear yellow. When the leaves fall, tiny orange-yellow capsules split and masses of orange-red berries are abundant. These vivid berries remain throughout most of the winter, where they contrast with the winter landscape. Bittersweet is a vigorous climber and will require trimming once established.

Hydrangea, trumpet vine, and clematis are rapid growing flowering vines that will wrap their way along the rustic sides and scramble across the twig roof. Or how about a rose-covered summer house? Be sure to take into account the location of your structure, as well as your temperature zone when seeking advice from a nursery or garden guidebook. If your summer house is in an exposed area, for example, it will probably be hit with an early frost. Whether or not you decide to add vines, your summer house is bound to be an attractive and welcome addition.

CHAPTER 4

Shelves & Planters

Hanging Plant Shelf

A garden should be rather small,
or you will have no fun at all.

REGINALD ARKELL

GATHER UP YOUR prize plants and set them on this willow-trimmed shelf. This versatile shelf is at home on a porch, along a picket fence, in a guest room, or on a kitchen wall. For old-fashioned charm, try weaving blue velvet ribbon through the willow loops and setting pots of lavender on the shelf. It makes a perfect perch for evergreen topiaries during winter celebrations. Attach it to the wall with sturdy pegs or hooks.

Twig accents are perfect for garden settings. A May basket on a doorknob gives a springtime welcome, inside or out.

A sundial on a twig stand will let you know when it's time to stop for the day.

The Willy Loveseat is a garden classic. Combine it with the Garden Chair and give weary gardeners a place to sit and survey their flowery kingdoms.

The angular design of this chair lends a sense of order to the riotous garden background.

The Tree Chair gives you a place to hang your hat while the crazy quilt seat cover adds a welcome splash of color to any room.

The Gothic Armchair uses the quirks and curves of the tree to full advantage. Search carefully to find just the right twigs for this project.

A yard sale rocker, rescued from oblivion and given a new lease on life with a twig seat, makes a handsome addition to any garden setting.

The handy drawer makes it easy to clean the house in preparation for next year's occupants.

A birdbath of twigs and recycled materials is simple to make.

The Birch and Copper Feeder and the Willow Log Cabin will help make your garden a haven for birds.

Turn your yard into a full service bird habitat with the Cabin Birdfeeder and the Stockade Shelter.

Bent willow and wire screening form a charming and simple picnic cover.

The openwork design of this basket makes it perfect for gathering delicate herbs without bruising them.

This folded bark envelope makes a lovely posy pocket.

These simple fences keep feet out of the vegetable patch and tangles of flowers from taking over in their exuberance.

The canopy frame is deceptively simple to build with its forks forming natural supports.

The Canopy Bench gives weary gardeners a place to relax as well as respite from sun and rain with its handsome striped canvas top.

The bench seat is padded and covered in durable canvas. You can also make a seat with a stone slab or a wood plank.

CUTTING CHART

NAME OF PART	QUANTITY	DIAMETER (INCHES)	LENGTH (INCHES)	DESCRIPTION
Hangers A	2	¼	17	forked
Border trim	13	¼	14–17	pliable
Shelf	1	½"-thick	4½ × 25	pine, or scrap wood

TOOLS

- Clippers or garden shears
- Coping saw
- Marking pencil
- Work gloves
- Tack hammer
- Ruler or measuring tape
- Safety goggles

MATERIALS

You will need to use pliable branches such as willow, alder, or cedar. Lengths will vary from between 14" and 17", and branches should be ¼" in diameter. A ¼" thick wood plank, 4½" × 25" is required for the shelf. You will also need 1" finishing nails and 1" box nails.

DIRECTIONS

1. Drill and nail pliable twigs along the front edge of the shelf and one at each end, creating the border trim as shown in diagram 1. However, any variation of twig border placement is possible.
2. Drill and nail two hangers to the back edge of the shelf 2" in from each end using 1" galvanized box nails (diagram 2).

Diagram 1

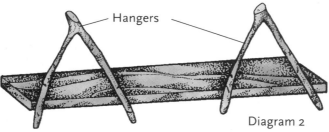

Hangers

Diagram 2

Picture Frame Shelf

*A display of orchids is like a floral
fancy-dress ball.*

E. M. HARDINGE, 1894

THIS VIRGINIA creeper–wrapped frame shelf was inspired by fragrant herbs and scented geraniums peeking out behind some discarded picture frames at an old farmhouse. It will provide support for a pot of trailing grape ivy resting on its shelf, or a vase of fresh picked garden flowers.

MATERIALS

Use such woods as willow, beech, or hickory for the basic frame. Lengths will vary from 14" to 22" with ¾" diameters. Two 18" supple willow branches are needed for the shelf trim along with an assortment of green (pliable) vines

CUTTING CHART

NAME OF PART	QUANTITY	DIAMETER (INCHES)	LENGTH (INCHES)	DESCRIPTION
Top/bottom rail A	2	¾	14	hardwood
Side rail B	2	¾	17	hardwood
Top/bottom rail C	2	¾	17	hardwood
Side rail D	2	¾	19	hardwood
Top/bottom rail E	2	¾	19	hardwood
Side rail F	2	¾	22	hardwood
Shelf brace	1	¼–¾	8–9	forked, hardwood
Shelf	1	1"-thick	6 × 10 semicircle	pine board
Shelf trim	1–2	¼–1	18	pliable

Vine frame wrap: one or two lengths of supple vine, as long as possible to wrap the frame. Use such vines as Dutchman's pipe, grapevine, honeysuckle, kudzu, and Virginia creeper.

TOOLS

• Single bit axe for felling trees	• Hand saw
• Garden shears or clippers	• Ruler
• Marking pencil	• Drill with a selection of bits
• Hammer	• Safety goggles
• Work gloves	

for the frame wrap. You will need a 1" thick slice of lumber approximately 6" × 10" for the shelf. Use galvanized common nails in assorted sizes, and finishing nails (¾", 1", and 1½") for the assembly.

DIRECTIONS

Cutting the Branches

1. Cut two ¾" diameter branches for the top/bottom rails A, each 14" long.
2. Cut two ¾" diameter branches for the side rails B, each 17" long.
3. Cut two ¾" diameter branches for the top/bottom rails C, each 17" long.
4. Cut two ¾" diameter branches for the side rails D, each 19" long.

5. Cut two ¾" diameter branches for the top/bottom rails E, each 19" long.

6. Cut two ¾" diameter branches for the side rails F, each 22" long.

7. Cut one ¼" to ¾" diameter forked branch for the shelf brace, 8" to 9" long.

8. Cut one or two ¼" to 1" diameter pliable branches for the shelf trim, 18" long.

9. Cut the supple vine to length as indicated on the cutting chart.

Assembling the Frame

1. Lay down side rails F, 13" apart and parallel, on the workbench.

2. Using the marking pencil, make a mark 4" from each end of both rails F. Lay the top and bottom rails E at the 4" marks. NOTE: Approximately 2" of rail E will extend beyond rail F (diagram 1).

3. Drill and nail top and bottom rails E to side rails F.

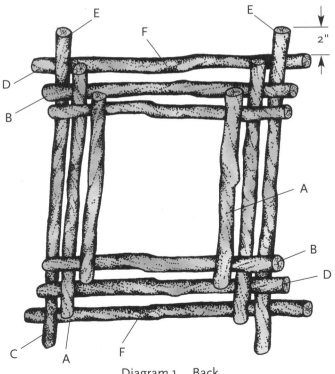

Diagram 1   Back

4. Lay side rails D across top and bottom rails E, 3" in from each end. (Side rails D should extend 2" beyond rails E at either end.) Drill and nail side rails D into rails E.

5. Lay top and bottom rails C across side rails D, 5¼" in from each end. (Rails C should extend 2" beyond rails D at either end.) Drill and nail top and bottom rails C into rails D.

6. Lay side rails B across top and bottom rails C, 4" in from each end (Side rails B should extend 2" beyond rails C at either end.) Drill and nail side rails B into rails C.

7. Lay top and bottom rails A across side rails B directly over top and bottom rails C. (Rails A should extend 2" beyond rails B at either end.) Drill and nail top and bottom rails A into rails B.

Adding the Shelf

1. The semicircle shelf is nailed to the bottom rail E from the back.

2. Position the shelf brace as shown in diagram 2. Nail the brace to the underside of the shelf and the bottom rail A, using finishing nails.

3. Carefully bend the shelf trim around the outside edge of the shelf. Nail the trim to the edge of the shelf with pilot holes and finishing nails.

4. Refer to the drawing on page 84 to wrap and weave the vine along the extended frame parts. At this point, the vine usually has a mind of its own, and somehow it finds its way along the extended branches.

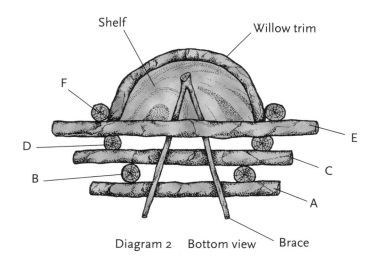

Diagram 2   Bottom view

SKILL LEVEL: EXPERIENCED

Rustic Etagere

Ah, well September,
the garden is still soft and green,
rinse out the flower pots,
and get them clean.

MARY SCRIBNER, 1873

DESIGNED TO BE PRACTICAL and sturdy, the shelf unit is easy to construct with ¾" thick pine boards and 6 ft. long poles. Once you learn the technique, you will probably want to build a wall of shelves, or combine several to fit any space. This 5 ft. wide, 5 ft. 8" high unit is ideal in a potting shed or outdoor protected area for storing flower pots, potting soil, and harvest trugs, while the extended branches serve as hooks for hanging hand tools, garden gloves, and accessories.

CUTTING CHART

NAME OF PART	QUANTITY	DIAMETER (INCHES)	LENGTH (INCHES)	DESCRIPTION
Shelves A	7	6¾-wide	60	pine board
Back supports B	3	one-by-four	68	pine
Upright poles C	5	¾–2	68–80	hardwood branches

TOOLS

- Single bit axe for felling trees
- Clippers or garden shears
- Pencil
- Safety goggles
- Electric drill and bit to accommodate three Phillips-head screws, or a Phillips-head screwdriver

- Crosscut saw
- Ruler or measuring tape
- Hammer
- Work gloves
- Level

MATERIALS

Seven ¾" thick pine boards, 5 ft. long and 6¾" wide. Three one-by-four boards 68" long for the back supports. Five hardwood (beech, birch, or maple) poles, in lengths ranging from 68" to 80" including extended branches, and ¾" to 2" in diameter. 2" to 4" galvanized nails are required. NOTE: The size of the nails is determined by the diameter of the poles. 1½" Phillips-head drywall screws are used to fasten the back supports to the shelves.

DIRECTIONS

Cutting the Shelves

With the crosscut saw cut all ¾" pine boards (shelves) to length (60"). These can be cut to length at the lumber yard.

NOTE: Shelves may be left natural, painted, or stained as desired. If you choose to paint or stain them, do so before construction begins.

Building the Shelves

1. Lay the seven shelves on edge on the floor, spaced as follows:

8"
8"
9"
10"
11"
13"
3¾"

NOTE: The back supports are added to the shelves while the shelves remain spaced on the floor.

2. Lay the back support B on top of all the back edges of the shelves A.
3. Lay the three one-by-four back supports across the back edges of the seven shelves.
4. Start by drilling two ⅛" diameter holes at the top of each back support.

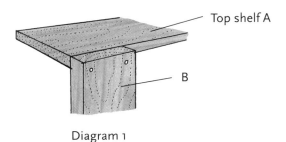

Top shelf A

B

Diagram 1

5. With the top of each back support flush with the top of the top shelf, the middle one centered 30" from each end of the shelf and the other two at the very ends of the shelf, screw the back supports into the shelves with two Phillips-head drywall screws each.
6. Continue screwing the back supports to the shelves. Carefully space all seven shelves using the dimensions in step 1. NOTE: These dimensions are

clear dimensions between the underside of one shelf and the top of the next. There should be a 3¾" space under the bottom shelf when you are done.

Raising the Shelves and Adding the Twig Uprights

NOTE: At this point it is helpful to have assistance. You and a helper can now raise the unit to its standing position. Have your helper hold the unit steady as you proceed.

1. Arrange the front/center upright C along the front of the shelves as pictured in diagram 3. Make sure the pole easily touches each shelf at each junction point. When you are satisfied with the placement, drill ⅛" diameter holes through the upright pole C where it meets each shelf. NOTE: It is important to maintain the same shelf spacing as at the back braces.

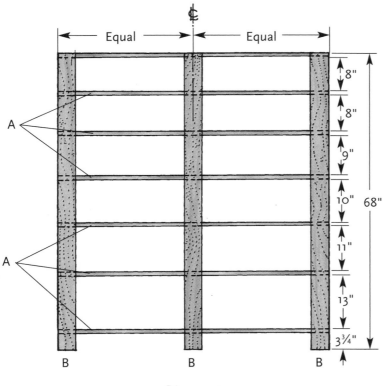

Diagram 2

2. Using galvanized nails, join the upright pole C to the shelves.

3. Repeat with the right and left front upright poles C, as in steps 1 and 2 above.

4. Nail on the remaining right and left back poles C in the same manner.

5. Clip all protruding lower branches.

6. Use the level to make sure the shelves are straight. Cut the bottoms of the poles as necessary.

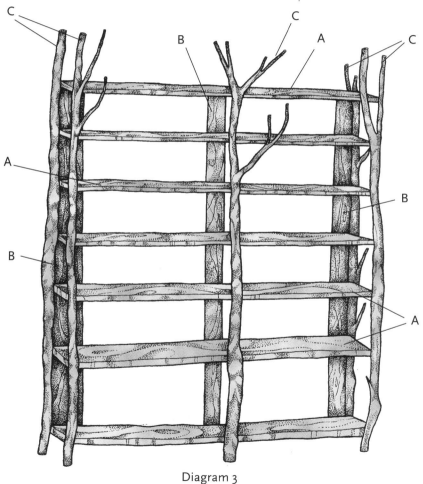

Diagram 3

Plant
Whatnot

When I pick or crush in my hand a twig of bay,
or brush against a bunch of rosemary,
or tread upon a tuft of thyme,
or pass through incense-laden Cistus,
I feel that here is all that is best
and purest and most refined,
and nearest to poetry.

GERTRUDE JEKYLL

SKILL LEVEL: INTERMEDIATE

MEMORIES OF GRANDMOTHER'S whatnot shelves combine with rustic twigs to create this shelf unit for displaying favorite plants. With its open shelves and corner design it can be used indoors near a window, or in any sheltered outdoor location. While you can probably find a spot for this piece almost anywhere, it seems just perfect for a kitchen corner where fragrant herbs can mingle with seasonal flowers and early spring seedlings.

CUTTING CHART

NAME OF PART	QUANTITY	DIAMETER (INCHES)	LENGTH (INCHES)	DESCRIPTION
Back leg A	1	$1\frac{1}{4}$	50	straight, hardwood
Front legs B	2	$1\frac{1}{4}$	46	straight, hardwood
Top beams C and D	4	$\frac{3}{4}$	14	straight, hardwood
Long braces F	2	$\frac{1}{2}$	36	straight, hardwood
Short braces G	2	$\frac{1}{4}-\frac{1}{2}$	18	straight, hardwood
Brace trim H	8	$\frac{1}{4}-\frac{1}{2}$	$2\frac{1}{4}-2\frac{1}{2}$	straight, pliable
Shelf E1,E2,E3 & E4	4		$14 \times 19\frac{1}{2}$	$\frac{1}{2}$" pine

TOOLS

- Single bit axe for felling trees
- Clippers or garden shears
- Marking pencil
- Hammer
- Carpenter's level (optional)
- Work gloves
- Crosscut hand saw
- Ruler or measuring tape
- $\frac{3}{8}$" variable-speed drill
- Sharp pocket knife
- Safety goggles

MATERIALS

You will want to choose straight branches for the legs and braces. Lengths will range from 14" to 50" and diameters from $\frac{1}{4}$" to $1\frac{1}{4}$". You'll need four pieces of $\frac{1}{2}$" thick pine (or similar wood) for the shelves, each 14" × 20". You will also need a selection of galvanized box nails, #2p, #4p, and #6p, along with finishing nails. Sandpaper may be required for the shelves.

DIRECTIONS

Making the Shelves

1. The shelves are triangular $\frac{1}{2}$" thick white pine measuring $19\frac{1}{2}$" across the front and 14" along the sides (diagram 1). NOTE: Other woods such as walnut, cherry, or oak may be used for shelves. Cut the four shelves roughly to size, allowing an extra $\frac{1}{8}$" all around for finishing. Lightly sand all shelves, if necessary.

2. Cut a 1" square notch in the back corner of each shelf to fit the back leg.

Cutting the Branches

1. Cut one straight 1¼" diameter branch for the back leg A, 50" long.
2. Cut two straight 1¼" diameter branches for the front legs B, each 46" long.
3. Cut four straight ¾" diameter branches for the beams C, each 14" long.
4. Cut two straight ½" diameter branches for the long braces F, each 36" long.
5. Cut two straight ¼" to ½" diameter branches for the short braces G, each 18" long.
6. Cut eight straight and pliable ¼" diameter branches for the beam trim H, each 2¼" to 2½" long. NOTE: Pliable branches are easier to install, and the lengths are adjusted during construction to ensure a tight fit.

Marking the Branches (Legs)

1. On the inside edge of each branch (leg), make a pencil mark 8" up from the bottom.
2. Make another pencil mark 10" above the first marks. Continue to mark the legs, each 10" above the one before, until you have marked four locations along the inside edge of each of the three legs A and B.
3. On the inside edge of each front leg B, make a pencil mark 3½" down from the top and a second mark 3" below that.
4. On the outside edge of the back leg A, make two pencil marks, one on each side, 5" down from the top and two more marks 3" below those.

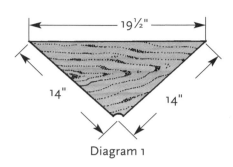

Diagram 1

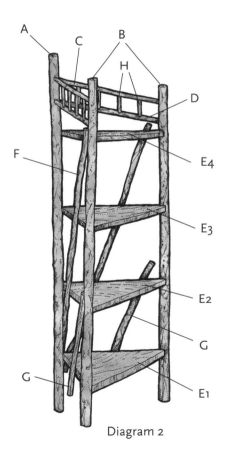

Diagram 2

Building the Stand

1. Use a sharp knife (or clippers) to angle the end of one top beam C to approximately one-third of its diameter. Butt C against leg A at the top pencil mark (5" down from the top) and check for a tight fit. Drill a pilot hole through the end of C and partway into A, and nail C to A.
2. Butt top beam C against front leg B at the top pencil mark (3½" down from the top). Angle the end of C, as above. Check for a tight fit. Drill a pilot hole through C and B and nail them together (diagram 4).

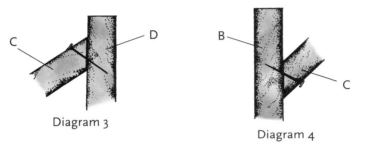

Diagram 3

Diagram 4

3. Butt top beam D against leg A at the pencil mark 3" down from top beam C. Angle the end, and check for a tight fit. Join D to A.
4. Repeat step 2 with top Beam D, nailing it to leg B. NOTE: Make sure both top beams are parallel.
5. Repeat step 1 with the second top beam C, on the opposite side against back leg A. NOTE: The angle formed by the top beams C and D nailed on either side of leg A must be the same as that of the back corner of the shelves.
6. Repeat step 2 with the opposite front leg B.
7. Angle, butt, drill, and nail the second top beam D against front leg B at the 3" pencil mark, and parallel to top beam C.

Adding the Shelves

1. Beginning with the lowest shelf E1, arrange the 19½" side squarely between the two front legs B, and the back leg A at the first pencil marks, and check for a tight fit. Trim the shelf to fit, if necessary. Drill pilot holes through B and A at the pencil marks, and partway through the shelves,

nailing only three-quarters of the way through. Leave one-quarter of the nail exposed until the construction is completely assembled. This prevents the driven nails from being loosened as you proceed.

2. Repeat step 1 above, fitting, drilling, and nailing the remaining three shelves in place at the pencil marks, working from the bottom up. Be careful when drilling and nailing, making certain that the shelves are level as you proceed.

Adding the Braces and Trim

1. With the back of the assembly facing you, lay one long brace F diagonally along the shelves, beginning approximately 5" from the bottom of the back leg A, slanted toward the top of the front shelf. This brace is nailed to the edge of the top shelf approximately 2" from the front leg (diagram 5). The long brace is attached to all four shelves at their junction. Repeat with the other long brace on the opposite side.

2. Lay the short braces G diagonally along the bottom two shelves E1 and E2 as shown in diagram 5. Nail them to the shelves as above.

3. Evenly space pencil marks along the top beams C and D, on either side of A approximately 3" apart. Fit brace trim pieces H between top beams C and D at the 3" pencil marks. Trim pieces H to fit if necessary. Drill and nail in place from the top of beam C and bottom of the beam D.

Diagram 5 Back view

Finishing

Hammer the exposed nails into place. Check the construction, and adjust the legs if necessary so that the shelves are balanced. Shelves may be left in their natural state or finished with linseed oil or paint. If you choose paint, it would be wise to paint before installation.

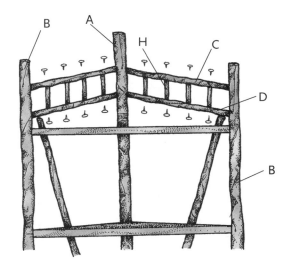

Diagram 6

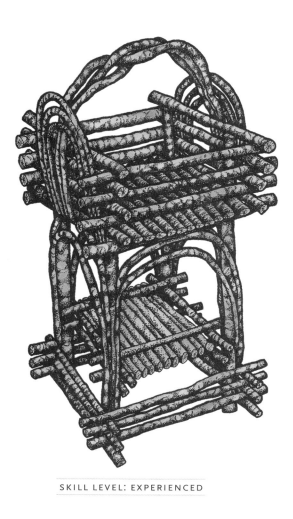

Standing Box Planter

*Especially should a small garden,
I think, be full of sweet scented flowers;
it gives them a loveable, intimate quality.*

LOUISE BEEBE WILDER

GARDEN CHARM is promised year round with this two level planter. Don't let the number of twigs frighten you. Learning these techniques will help you with larger projects, and hopefully inspire you to create your own designs. Cascading with dainty blooms, the standing planter is the perfect welcome beside any front door. Use its sturdy handle to carry it inside at the first sign of frost to brighten up a winter room.

CUTTING CHART

NAME OF PART	QUANTITY	DIAMETER (INCHES)	LENGTH (INCHES)	DESCRIPTION
Legs A	4	1¼	28	hardwood
Top rails B	16	¾	18	hardwood
Lower rails C	10	¾	15	hardwood
Bottom rails D	14	¾	18	hardwood
Platforms E	24	½–¾	17	hardwood
Handles	3	½	40	pliable
Top horseshoe trim	6	¼	22–30	pliable
Lower horseshoe trim	4	½	40	pliable

TOOLS

- Single bit axe for felling trees
- Clippers or garden shears
- Marking pencil
- Hammer
- Work gloves
- Crosscut hand saw
- Ruler or measuring tape
- ⅜" variable-speed drill
- Safety goggles

MATERIALS

You will need sixty ¾" diameter twigs, ranging in length from 15" to 18" for the basic structure; four 1¼" diameter branches, 28" long for the legs; and twenty-four ½" to ¾" diameter branches for the platforms. You will also need an assortment of ¼" and ½" diameter pliable branches, from 22" to 40" long for the horseshoe trim and the handles. Galvanized common nails in assorted sizes (#4p, #6p, and #8p) and about four dozen finishing nails will also be necessary.

DIRECTIONS

Cutting the Branches

1. Cut four 1¼" diameter branches for the legs A, each 28" long.
2. Cut sixteen ¾" diameter branches for the top rails B, each 18" long.
3. Cut ten ¾" diameter branches for the middle rails C, each 15" long.

4. Cut fourteen ¾" diameter branches for the bottom rails D, each 18" long.
5. Cut twenty-four ½" to ¾" diameter branches for the two platforms E, each 17" long.
6. Cut three ½" diameter pliable branches for the handles, each 40" long.
7. Cut six ¼" diameter pliable branches each from 22" to 30" long, for the top horseshoe.
8. Cut four ½" diameter pliable branches for the lower horseshoe trim, each 40" long.

Laying Out the Sub-Assembly

1. All of the rails are joined in the familiar log-cabin pattern at the top of the legs, by assembling alternating parallel branches at right angles (diagram 1). With a pencil, make a mark 7" from the top of all four legs. Nail one top rail B to the leg A at this point, first drilling a pilot hole. Allowing 3" of the rail to extend beyond both legs, nail the rail to the next leg in the same manner, at the 7" mark. The legs should be 11" apart.
2. Repeat step 1 above with the remaining two legs and one rail.
3. Lay two rails B across the first two rails, against the outside of the legs and extending 3" beyond each leg, to form a square. Nail the beams to the legs from the outside.

Laying Out the Top Platform

Arrange approximately eleven platform parts E across the second pair of rails, allowing about 2" to overhang both rails. Nail the platforms to the rails at each junction.

Building the Box

1. Lay two more rails B across the platform parts and the outside leg rails, against the legs. Nail to the rail beneath it at all four corners near the legs.
2. Lay ten more rails, outside the legs, across each pair of rails beneath, and nail in place to the rails beneath.

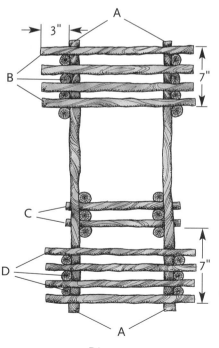

Diagram 1

Building the Middle Rails and the Lower Platform

1. Turn the assembly upside down and lay one middle rail C across the inside of two legs at a location approximately 7" from the bottom. Drill pilot holes and nail in place.
2. Repeat with the opposite side.
3. Turn the assembly upright again and arrange approximately thirteen lower platform branches E across the two parallel middle rails C, allowing 2" to extend at either end. Nail the platform branches to the rails at each junction.
4. Place the remaining six middle rails C, one pair across another, inside the legs. Nail each rail in place to the rail beneath it.

Adding the Bottom Rails

1. Lay one bottom rail D across two bottom legs A (as close to the bottom as possible). Drill pilot holes and nail in place.
2. Repeat step 1 on the opposite side.
3. Lay another pair of bottom rails D across the pair of rails just installed, on the outside of the legs. Drill pilot holes and nail them to the rails beneath.
4. Continue to build, log-cabin fashion, with the remaining bottom rails D.

Adding Bottom Trim

1. Refer to diagram 3 for the lower horseshoe trim placement. Carefully bend one 40" pliable branch into an arch. Place one end against the outside of one leg and carefully bring it up, arching it and bringing it down along the leg on the opposite side, ending it just above the bottom stave. Drill and nail in place using finishing nails.
2. Repeat with the three remaining sides. NOTE: The lower horseshoe trim is applied to the four sides, while the top trim and the handle are attached to two sides.
3. To form the interior lower horseshoe trim, carefully

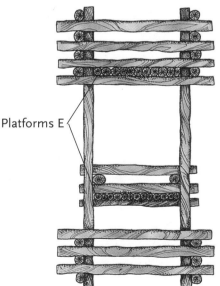

Platforms E

Diagram 2

bend one 36" pliable twig, and using the same method as above, nail the horseshoe to the leg, just inside the attached horseshoe.

Adding the Handles

1. Carefully bend one handle twig and place it against the outside of the lowest top rail B, and bring it up across the other three, allowing it to arch over the box approximately 25" high, bringing it down across the rails B on the opposite side. Drill and nail to two or three rails on both sides of the box.
2. Repeat with the remaining two handle parts, carefully weaving them around the first handle (diagram 3).

Diagram 3   Side, with handle and bottom trim

Adding the Top Horseshoe Trim

Refer to diagram 4 for the top horseshoe trim placement. To form the trim, gently bend each pliable twig in place, and using the same method described in *Adding Bottom Trim,* nail three horseshoe trims in place along the sides, and on top of the handles.

Diagram 4   Side, adding horseshoe trim

Window Box

SKILL LEVEL: BEGINNER

A little garden square and wall'd.

TENNYSON

IN THE PAST window boxes were used mostly by city dwellers, as a way to make a garden of the smallest porch or windowsill. Today, window box planters are used indoors as well as outside, adding color, texture, and scent to any number of settings. Filled with potted plants, this twig box is the perfect centerpiece for your picnic table, or heap it with vegetables for your harvest feast. To use it as a traditional window box outdoors, it will have to be supported on four sturdy brackets or rest on a shelf, if the windowsill is narrow.

103

CUTTING CHART

NAME OF PART	QUANTITY	DIAMETER (INCHES)	LENGTH (INCHES)	DESCRIPTION
Front/back rails A	12	½–¾	22–25	hardwood
End rails B	10	½–¾	8–11	hardwood
Bottom rails C	15–20	½–¾	8½	hardwood
Handles D	4	½	22–30	pliable
Horseshoe trim E	12	¼–½	12–18	pliable

TOOLS

- Crosscut hand saw
- Drill and bit
- Marking pencil
- Safety goggles
- Garden shears or clippers
- Ruler
- Hammer
- Work gloves

MATERIALS

You will need 36 twigs of any wood, ranging in length from 8" to 25" with diameters from ½" to ¾" for the window box. You will also need flexible ½" diameter branches, from 15" to 30" long for the horseshoe trim and the handles; and 1" galvanized finishing nails.

DIRECTIONS

Cutting the Window Box Branches

1. Refer to the Cutting Chart and Assembly Diagrams. Mark the parts as you cut them to speed up the assembly process. A good way to do this is with a strip of masking tape that can be removed easily.

   All the following branch diameters are ½" to ¾".
2. Cut two 22" branches for the front/back rails A.
3. Cut two 22½" branches for the front/back rails A1.
4. Cut two 23" branches for the front/back rails A2.
5. Cut two 23½" branches for the front/back rails A3.
6. Cut two 24" branches for the front/back rails A4.
7. Cut two 25" branches for the front/back rails A5.

8. Cut two 8" branches for the end rails B.
9. Cut two 9" branches for the end rails B1.
10. Cut two 9½" branches for the end rails B2.
11. Cut two 10" branches for the end rails B3.
12. Cut two 11" branches for the end rails B4.
13. Cut fourteen 8½" branches for the bottom rails C.

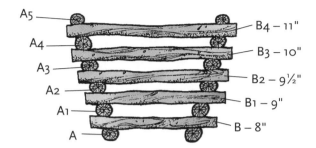

Diagram 1 Assembly diagram showing end rails B

Building the Bottom

1. The log-cabin design is built by alternating rails A and B; the slight variation in the length of the rails is required to create the window box shape.
2. Begin by laying two rails A parallel on the workbench. At approximately 3" from either end of the rails, arrange the fourteen bottom rails C across the two parallel rails A. Drill pilot holes through the bottom rails into the two rails A and nail them in place.

Constructing the Box (see diagrams 1 and 2)

1. Begin by nailing one end rail B across each end of the two parallel rails A. (These will lay at either end of the row of bottom rails and parallel to them.)
2. Lay one front/back rail A1 across the end rails B. Nail in place.
3. Repeat on opposite side.
4. Lay one end rail B1 across the ends of rails A1. Nail in place.
5. Repeat the above procedure until the remaining front/back rails, A2, A3, A4, and A5, and the remaining end rails, B2, B3, and B4, are nailed in place as shown in diagrams 1 and 2. The structure should flare out slightly as each layer is added.

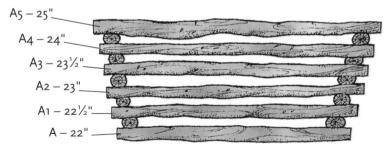

Diagram 2 Assembly diagram showing front/back rails A

Adding the Handles

1. Carefully bend one 30" long pliable twig. Place one end of the twig against the inside of both front/back rails A along the outside of the end rails B. Bring it up along the front/back rails, forming an arch at 5" above the end rail B4, and bringing it down along the inside edge of the rails A on the opposite side. Drill and nail in place where the handle meets the side rails, using galvanized finishing nails (diagram 3).
2. Repeat with the opposite end of the window box.
3. Using the same method as above, attach one 22" pliable handle part inside the attached handle, forming the double handle.
4. Repeat with the opposite end of the window box.

Adding the Horseshoe Trim

1. Refer to diagram 3 for horseshoe trim placement. To form the outside trim, carefully bend one 18" pliable twig. Place one end of E against the inside of the bottom end rail B and bring it up across the front/back rails, arching it and bringing it down across the front/back rails again, allowing it to rest between two bottom rails C. Drill and nail in place using finishing nails.
2. To form the inside horseshoe trim, carefully bend one 12" pliable twig, and using the same method as above, nail the horseshoe in place inside the attached horseshoe.
3. Repeat with the remaining horseshoes, creating three pairs for each side.

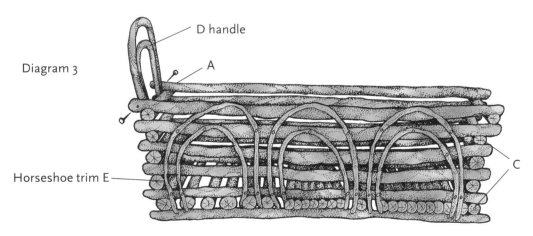

Diagram 3

D handle

A

Horseshoe trim E

C

Trellis Wall Planter

*Springtime is advancing up the valleys
and slopes of the northern hills …*

CALVIN COOLIDGE

SITTING ON A TABLE, or hanging on the wall, this 10" square planter with attached trellis support is a dramatic accent to hold your favorite plants and flowers. It is perfect for ivy winding, as well as for trailing plants such as creeping fig, jasmine, or philodendron. Whether you use it for nasturtiums on the porch or creeping rosemary in the kitchen, you will probably want to make several.

CUTTING CHART				
NAME OF PART	QUANTITY	DIAMETER (INCHES)	LENGTH (INCHES)	DESCRIPTION
Planter parts A	23	¾	10	straight sticks
Trellis parts B	7	¼–½	24	pliable twigs
Trellis brace C	1	¼–½	20	pliable twig

TOOLS	
• Hand saw	• Clippers or garden shears
• Drill and bit	• Ruler
• Pencil	• Hammer
• Safety goggles	• Work gloves

MATERIALS

You will need 23 sticks of any wood, 10" long and ¾" in diameter for the planter. You will also need 8 pliable twigs, such as willow, each 24" long and ¼" to ½" in diameter for the trellis. Finishing nails or wire brads (finishing nails without a head) are used in the construction.

DIRECTIONS

Cutting the Sticks and Twigs

1. Cut 23 sticks, ¾" in diameter, for the main planter parts A, each 10" long.
2. Cut 7 pliable twigs, ¼" to ½" in diameter, for the trellis parts B, each 24" long.
3. Cut 1 pliable twig, ¼" to ½" in diameter, for the trellis brace C, 20" long.

Drilling the Sticks

1. With a pencil, make a mark 1" from both ends of all sticks A.
2. Drill a pilot hole large enough to accommodate your finishing nails through each of the 46 pencil marks.

Building the Bottom

1. Arrange two sticks A, approximately 10" apart and parallel on the work

table. Lay one side stick A at right angles across the two parallel sticks, making sure that the pre-drilled pilot holes line up. NOTE: All right angle parts extend approximately 1" on either side. Nail in place.

2. Repeat with the opposite end.
3. Approximately 2" from each attached twig, center three twigs A across the parallel twigs. Nail in place.

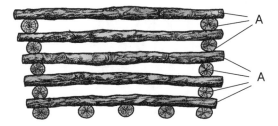

Diagram 1 Front

Building the Planter

1. The planter is built by alternating parts A in a log-cabin building manner. The sticks are nailed in place at an angle to prevent nails from hitting nails. Side parts should parallel the bottom.
2. Begin by laying a stick across the four bottom side twigs. Nail in place, at an angle, using finishing nails.
3. Repeat on the opposite side.
4. Repeat the above procedure until all parts A are used, forming a box (diagram 1).

Adding the Trellis

1. Begin adding the trellis twigs B from the center. Using pilot holes, nail the center trellis twig to the bottom and top planter sticks.
2. Add the neighboring trellis twigs with the top ends fanned out, using the same method as above.
3. Carefully bend trellis brace C. Place C across the seven standing trellis twigs approximately 8" from the top. Drill and nail in place where C meets the seven parts B (diagram 2).

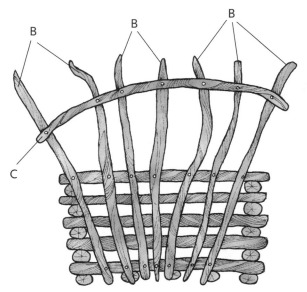

Diagram 2 Back view

Plant Pedestal

I got a large round of thick green moss,
and some strawberry-vines mingled with it,
and a delicate little fern to plant
right in the center...

MRS. JULIA MCNAIR WRIGHT, 1883

THIS NATURAL PLANT STAND, tall and stately, can make any corner feel like a country garden, whether it's the winter parlor or summer porch. The center shelf guarantees stability, while serving as the perfect perch for trailing plants. Try some unusual ivy varieties such as gnome, spetchley, or Irish lace.

C U T T I N G   C H A R T

NAME OF PART	QUANTITY	DIAMETER (INCHES)	LENGTH (INCHES)	DESCRIPTION
Legs A & B	8	¾	46	hardwood/pliable
Platform C	1	1¾-thick	8 × 8 square	lumber/pliable
Center platform D	1	1¾-thick	6 × 6 square	lumber/pliable
Braces E	4	½	8½	hardwood/pliable

T O O L S

• Single bit axe for felling trees	• Crosscut hand saw
• Clippers or garden shears	• Ruler or measuring tape
• Marking pencil	• Drill with a selection of bits
• Hammer	• Safety goggles
• Work gloves	

MATERIALS

Any pliable hardwood (such as willow, beech, birch, cherry, or hickory) may be used. The branches need to be flexible to permit slight bending during construction. You will need eight 46" lengths, ¾" diameter; four 8½" lengths, ½" diameter; and two 1¾" thick pieces of scrap wood.

DIRECTIONS

Cutting the Branches

1. Cut eight ¾" diameter branches for legs A, each 46" long.
2. Cut four ½" diameter branches for the braces E, each 8½" long.

Laying Out the Sub-Assembly

1. Place the platform B on the workbench. Refer to diagram 4 for placement of legs A, and mark the location for the four legs.

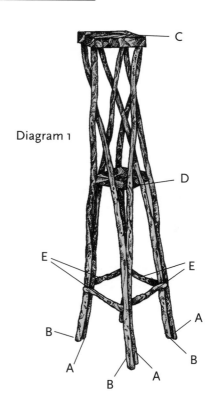

Diagram 1

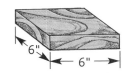

Diagram 2 Center platform D

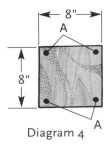

Diagram 4

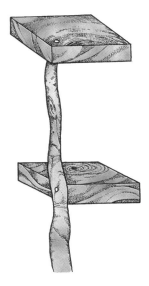

Diagram 6

2. With pilot holes, nail one leg to the underside of the platform.
3. Nail the attached leg to a corner of the center platform as shown in diagram 6.
4. Repeat leg-to-platform-to-center platform installation with the three remaining legs A.

Attaching Legs B
1. Refer to diagram 5. Using a pencil, mark B locations. With pilot hole and nail, attach one leg B in place.
2. Carefully bend leg B and attach to the center platform at a slant, under the corner leg A (refer to diagram 7).
3. Repeat steps 1 and 2 above with the remaining three legs B.

Adding the Braces
1. Mark a location 8" from the bottom of legs A.
2. Butt one brace E between two legs A at the 8" mark. Nail in place with pilot holes. NOTE: The braces are butted between the A legs, and are outside the B legs.
3. Continue to butt, drill, and nail the remaining three braces in place, as in step 2.

Make sure your plant pedestal stands straight. Trim the legs, if needed.

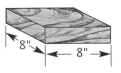

Diagram 3   Top

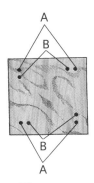

Diagram 5

Diagram 7

Twig & Vine Planter

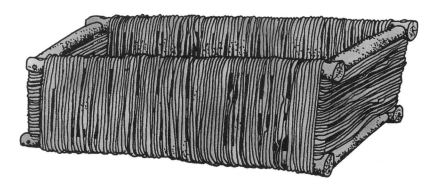

Where'er you tread,
the blushing flow'rs rise,
and all things flourish
where you turn your eyes.

ALEXANDER POPE

THIS RUSTIC twig and vine planter is the ideal setting for a rampant and wild display. Lined with rich green moss, the planter will be a showpiece in your garden, along a path, on a porch, or outside a front gate. You will also have the pleasure of gathering your building materials in the woods and getting in the mood for a bit of wild gardening when you decide to build this twig and vine planter.

		CUTTING	CHART	
NAME OF PART	QUANTITY	DIAMETER (INCHES)	LENGTH (INCHES)	DESCRIPTION
Beams A	4	1	32	straight
Spacers B	8	¾	9½	straight
Side rails C	4	¾	10	straight
Plant box supports D	3	¾	9½	straight
Side braces E	2	¾	9½	straight

TOOLS

- Crosscut hand saw
- Staple gun (optional)
- Marking pencil
- Hammer•
- Garden shears or clippers
- Ruler or measuring tape
- Safety goggles
- Work gloves
- Screwdriver (optional, if using screws to assemble the piece)
- #2 Robertson or Phillips bit (optional, if using screws)
- Drill (electric or hand) and a selection of bits

MATERIALS

You will need 21 twigs of any wood such as willow, beech, birch, or dogwood, ranging in length from 9" to 32" and with diameters from ¾" to 1". You will also need a selection of supple vines such as honeysuckle, grapevine, or hops, along with enough moss or other suitable lining for the bottom and sides of the box. NOTE: Coconut mat is a manufactured layering product available at most nurseries and garden centers. You might also consider building the box around a plastic liner and adjusting the measurements to fit. To assemble the box you will need galvanized flathead nails in assorted sizes (#4p, #6p, and #8p) or thirty #6 screws. Use a hammer and staples (or staple gun) to secure the vines where needed. If you want to hang the box you will need 8" to 10" steel shelf supports or decorative brackets available at home centers or flea markets.

DIRECTIONS

Cutting the Branches

1. Cut four 1" diameter branches for beams A, each 32" long.
2. Cut eight ¾" diameter branches for the spacers B, each 9½" long.
3. Cut four ¾" diameter branches for the side rails C, each 10" long.
4. Cut two ¾" diameter branches for the plant box supports D, each 9½" long.

Laying Out the Sub-Assembly

1. Butt one spacer B between two beams A, approximately 1" from the end of the beams. Drill pilot holes and nail in place. Place a second spacer at the opposite end of the two beams. Drill pilot holes and nail in place.
2. Repeat step 1 above with the remaining two beams A and two spacers B.
3. Butt one spacer between one set of spacers/beams at approximately 8" from the installed end spacer B. Drill and nail in place.
4. Repeat step 1 above with another spacer at approximately 8".
5. Repeat steps 3 and 4 with the remaining spacers B and the set of spacers/beams.

Joining the Sub-Assemblies

1. Butt one bottom side rail C between the two sub-assemblies. Drill and nail in place from the front of both beams. Repeat with the opposite side.
2. Butt one top side rail C between the two sub-assemblies. Drill and nail in place as above. Repeat with the remaining top rail.

Adding the Plant Box Supports and Side Braces

1. Using a pencil and ruler, mark equally spaced points, approximately 6" apart where the three plant box supports will be joined to both beams A. Drill pilot holes and nail in place as pictured.
2. From the lower inside corner of one end spacer, place a side brace E at an angle to the upper inside corner of the adjacent end spacer. Using pilot holes, nail in place. Repeat with the opposite side.

Adding the Vines

1. Wrap a length of vines over the top and bottom beams A. Check your progress as you go, keeping each wrap tight. Cinch the ends of each new length under the previous wrap and staple where necessary. Continue wrapping vines horizontally along the end spacers. Wrap vines tightly around the bottom beams and over the plant box supports.

2. To line the planter with moss, stuff the space between the vines from the inside. Start at the bottom and work up, packing the moss firmly in place. Use the largest piece of moss to create an even layer on the sides.

Diagram 1

Plant Suggestions

This box, lined with moss, suits any wild-looking flowers or foliage. Ivy, silver nettle, nasturtium, petunia, bidens, weigela, begonia, and helichrysum are just a few of the possibilities. For a lovely display try combining geraniums, silver nettle vine, lobelia, impatiens, bacopa, and verbena.

CHAPTER 5

Birdhouses & Feeders

SKILL LEVEL: INTERMEDIATE

I come from fields once tall with wheat,
from pastures deep in fern and thistle;
I come from vales of meadowsweet,
and I love to whistle.

E.B. WHITE

BIRD FEEDERS come in a surprising array of shapes and sizes. Nature enthusiasts and, more importantly, birds seem especially fond of this model. Easy enough to make in a day, you may want several to hang around your property or to give as gifts. Be sure to search the firewood pile for nicely marked logs and branches. Suspended from a tree limb or mounted on a post, this feeder blends gracefully with nature.

TOOLS	
• Crosscut hand saw	• Sandpaper (optional)
• Ruler or measuring tape	• Marking pencil
• Woodcarver's gouge and mallet	• Drill and a selection of bits
• Hammer	• Clippers or garden shears
• Safety goggles	• Work gloves
• Single bit axe for felling trees, if you don't have a wood pile	

MATERIALS

Choose two 6" diameter white birch slices, 1" thick for the top, and 2" thick for the bottom. NOTE: Any hardwood such as hickory, maple, or beech may be used. You will also need one 1½" diameter branch, 6" long for the center post. Four 1½" galvanized roofing nails and a screw-eye for hanging are also necessary.

DIRECTIONS

Begin by sanding on both sides of the top wood slice and only one side of the bottom slice.

Shaping the Feeder

NOTE: The gouge is a potentially dangerous hand tool. Wear heavy-duty work gloves and safety glasses to avoid cuts and flying wood chips.

1. With a dark pencil, mark a ½" margin around the circumference of the bottom wood slice.
2. Use the woodcarver's gouge and mallet to begin carving a depression across the middle. Turn the wood slice as you work and continue to carve at an angle from opposite sides, toward the center. Aim for a shallow angle along the rim with a concave bottom, 1½" deep in the middle.

Assembling the Feeder

1. Center the 6" long post on the underside of the 1" thick top slice. Using pilot holes and two nails, join the top piece to the post from the outside.

2. Position the 6" long center post in the base of the gouged-out bottom. Attach the two pieces from the bottom, using two nails and pilot holes to avoid splitting the wood.

3. Add a galvanized metal screw-eye centered in the top and a rope for hanging the feeder.

Bark Teepee Birdhouse

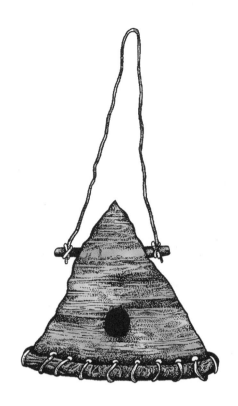

Make a place safe for birds and the birds will find it out and occupy it.

C.C. ABBOT

TEST YOUR BARK peeling skills with this charming 7" tall teepee, perfect for chickadees and house wrens. The 1⅛" diameter opening and lack of perch help to reduce the chances of sparrows using the hole or bothering the chicks. This classic North American design lends itself to indoor display, and can be made in a variety of sizes to grace shelves and window ledges.

T O O L S	
• Clippers or garden shears	• Ruler or measuring tape
• Pencil	• Scissors
• Leather hole punch or awl	• Large-eye needle and heavy thread

MATERIALS

You will need one sheet of peeled bark for the teepee, 8" wide and 1 ft. long, and one sheet of peeled bark for the teepee floor, approximately 8" × 8". You will also need a ¼" diameter supple willow shoot, 2 ft. long for forming the bottom rim; a 6" long straight branch and twine or rawhide for hanging; and peeled bark strips for lacing, ⅛" wide. Two pattern pieces, teepee pattern, and teepee floor pattern are provided. NOTE: To prepare the patterns, enlarge on a photocopier at the percentage given.

DIRECTIONS

Assembling the Teepee

1. Enlarge the teepee pattern on a photocopier (diagram 1), and use to trace the pattern onto the back of the bark. Cut out the teepee using scissors, and carefully form into the cone shape. NOTE: The edges overlap to form the teepee.

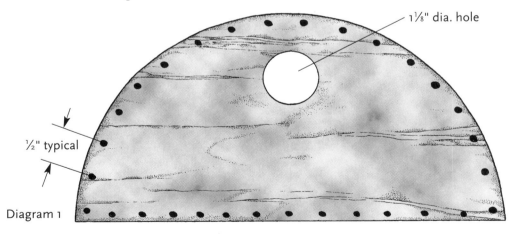

Teepee pattern. Enlarge this by 133% and take larger copy and further enlarge 200%.

2. Using the hole punch (or awl) punch holes evenly, approximately ½"
   apart along the overlapping edges. Using the ⅛" wide peeled bark strip,
   lace the teepee together through the punched holes (diagram 2). For increased strength, lace all parts together with the needle and heavy thread
   first, and then add the peeled bark.
3. Cut out a 1⅛" diameter opening on the front of the teepee (see pattern,
   diagram 1).
4. Enlarge the teepee floor pattern (diagram 3). Draw around the pattern
   on the back of the 8" × 8" piece of bark with a pencil. Cut out the teepee
   floor using scissors. Adjust the circumference, if necessary, to suit the
   large opening of the cone. Using the awl (or hole punch) punch holes
   evenly, approximately ½" to ¾" apart along the outside edge.
5. Carefully bend a 2 ft. long pliable willow shoot (or other supple branch)
   into a ring and fit it around the edge of the teepee floor. Using the peeled
   bark strip (or needle and heavy thread first) lace the willow shoot in
   place along the outside edge of the floor as in step 2 above (diagram 4).
6. Lace the floor to the teepee using the peeled bark strip.

Adding the Hanger

1. Punch a ¼" diameter hole in either side of the
   teepee approximately 1½" to 2" from the top. Place a
   straight ¼" diameter branch through the holes and
   tie twine or rawhide to the protruding ends to hang
   the finished teepee birdhouse.

Diagram 2

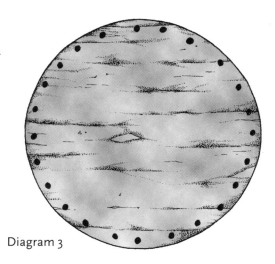

Diagram 3

Teepee floor pattern. Enlarge the pattern by
133% and take that copy and enlarge by 200%.

Diagram 4   Laced bottom

Willow Log Cabin Birdhouse

I hear the birds make music fit for angels…

ISLE OF INNISFREE, IRISH BALLAD

THIS BIRDHOUSE IS made from scrap plywood and willow twigs, and its galvanized tin roof helps to protect the birds in stormy weather. The drawer is an idea borrowed from bird cages, and is a functional element for cleaning out the house after the tenants have moved. You will need moderate carpentry skills to construct the basic cabin. If you're dubious about building it yourself, have someone skilled help you, or try nailing willow twigs on a purchased birdhouse.

• Crosscut hand saw	• Keyhole saw

• Table saw or band saw (optional)   NOTE: These are potentially dangerous tools and should be used only by an experienced operator who knows how to use them safely.

• Shears or clippers	• Ruler or measuring tape
• Marking pencil	• Hammer
• Safety goggles	• Work gloves

MATERIALS

The house size is approximately 5" × 5" × 8½" high.

One piece ½" pine board 6" × 3 ft. long, or an assortment of scrap wood for the basic house and drawer, along with carpenter's wood glue. You will also need an assortment of twigs with diameters of ¼" to ¾", and 7" long. Galvanized tin 8" × 1 ft. is required for the roof, along with galvanized box nails, ½" finishing nails, and one galvanized screw-eye for hanging. Seven pattern pieces for the front, back, sides, bottom, and drawer are provided. Photocopy them and use them to trace out the patterns.

DIRECTIONS

Cutting the Cabin

1. Photocopy all pattern pieces and cut them out. Using a pencil, trace all cabin pattern pieces on the ½" pine.
2. Using the saw, cut out one cabin bottom.
3. Cut out two cabin sides; on each piece, bevel one short edge at a 45-degree angle.
4. Cut out one cabin front; cut the entrance hole, using the keyhole saw.
5. Cut out one cabin back.

Cutting the Drawer

1. Using a pencil, trace all drawer pattern pieces on the ½" pine.
2. Using the saw, cut out one drawer bottom.
3. Cut out two drawer sides.
4. Cut out one drawer front.
5. Cut out one drawer back.

Building the Cabin

1. Nail the back to the edges of the sides with galvanized finishing nails or box nails. Put glue where the pieces meet before nailing, and be sure the edges are flush and even with each other. Also, be sure that the bevels on the side pieces are at the top of the cabin back and facing outward to match the slopes of the roof (diagram 1).

2. Nail the front to the edges of the sides with glue. Again, be sure the edges are flush and even (diagram 2).

3. With glue on the bottom edges of the front, back, and sides, nail the bottom piece in place.

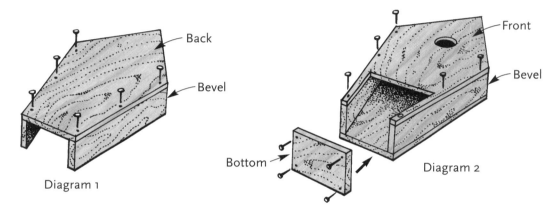

Diagram 1

Diagram 2

Diagram 3

Diagram 4

Building the Drawer

1. Apply glue to the back edge of the drawer bottom piece. Place the drawer back against it with the wider side up, making sure the edges are flush and square. Use two finishing nails to secure (diagram 3).

2. Place the drawer side pieces against the glued edges of the bottom and the back so they are flush. Use finishing nails to secure the side piece to the back and to the bottom (diagram 4).

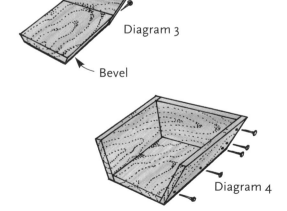

3. Apply glue to the ends of the side pieces, and the bottom. Place the drawer front, with the wider side up, against the drawer side edges flush with the bottom. Secure to bottom and sides with finishing nails (diagram 5).

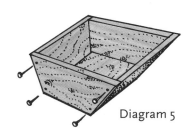

Diagram 5

Adding the "Logs"

1. Cover the face of the drawer with horizontal twigs. NOTE: The top-most twig should have a short branch for a "pull" (diagram 6).
2. Using the garden shears, cut and nail the ¼" to ¾" diameter twigs horizontally to the face of the cabin with finishing nails. To prevent splitting, drill pilot holes before nailing. Continue this on the back and sides (diagram 7).

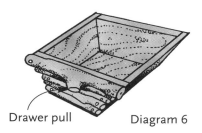

Drawer pull   Diagram 6

Adding the Tin Roof

1. Fold the 8" × 1 ft. galvanized tin in half to form the peaked roof. The roof overhangs the house approximately 2" along the sides and 1½" over the front and back. Arrange the roof over the house along the beveled edges, and drill holes for the galvanized box nails at the locations where the roof meets the edges of the house. Before nailing the roof in place, drill a hole midway along the ridge for the galvanized screw-eye. Drill a pilot hole midway along a ¾" diameter stick 1½" long. Place this under the roof ridge and screw the screw-eye through the tin into the stick (diagram 8).
2. Nail the roof in place over the cabin.
3. Hang the willow log cabin birdhouse from the screweye with a cord or leather thong.

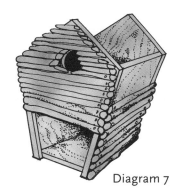

Diagram 7

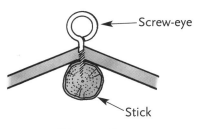

Screw-eye

Stick

Diagram 8

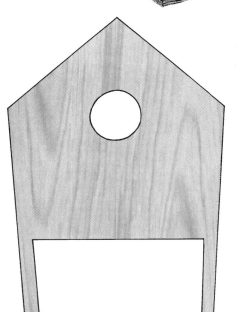

Enlarge patterns #1,
#2, and #3 by 133%,
then take the larger
copy and enlarge by
a further 200%.

#1   Front (cut 1)

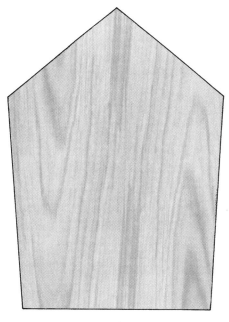

#2   Back (cut 1)

45° bevel

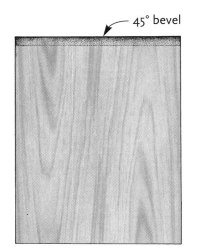

#3   Sides (cut 2)

#4   Bottom (cut 1)

Enlarge patterns #4, #5,
and #6 by 200%.

#5   Drawer front and
back (cut 2)

#6   Drawer sides (cut 2)

Laced Bark Birdhouse

SKILL LEVEL: INTERMEDIATE

For soon we reach a pleasant place
of once upon a time
Where birdies sing the hour of day,
and flowers talk in rhyme.

A.T. BROWN

INTERIOR DESIGN themes increasingly bring the outdoors inside with a host of decorative items, and birdhouses displayed as small works of art top the list of favorite rustic items. With its peeled bark, this charming model creates the illusion of a miniature woodland indoors, whether it's placed on the coffee table or used as a centerpiece for a special dinner. If you choose to hang it outdoors, you will provide shelter for nest-building families of wrens or chickadees, nuthatches or titmouses.

129

TOOLS

• Clippers or garden shears	• Ruler or measuring tape
• Marking pencil	• Scissors and sharp pocket knife
• Leather hole punch or awl	• Tack hammer
• Large-eye needle and heavy thread (optional)	• Work gloves

MATERIALS

You will need one 4" × 4" pine board ½" thick for the base and a selection of birch bark sheets: four 8" wide and 10" long for the sides, and four 10" wide and 7" long for the roof. You will also need a selection of straight branches such as willow, hickory, or maple, 5" to 10" long and ¾" in diameter to construct the birdhouse. Vine strips are used for lacing (heavy thread and a large-eye needle are optional for extra strength). Four galvanized roofing nails are used to attach the roof, ¾" carpet tacks to attach the bark to the base, and one galvanized eye-bolt, washer, and nut are used for hanging the birdhouse. You will also need heavy books or bricks for pressing the bark flat. Patterns are provided for the birdhouse sides and roof. Enlarge the patterns on a photocopier at the percentage given.

DIRECTIONS

Cutting the Bark Sheets

1. Place the flattened bark pieces, face down, on the work table. Using the enlarged pattern (diagram 1), trace the outline of the birdhouse side on the back of the bark. Using the scissors, cut out one house side.

2. Repeat step 1 on the three remaining birdhouse sides.

3. Choose one side for the front. Using the scissors or a sharp knife, cut out a 1¼" diameter entrance hole as the side pattern indicates.

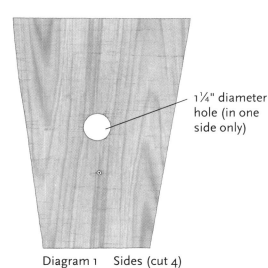

1¼" diameter hole (in one side only)

Diagram 1   Sides (cut 4)

4. Place the flattened bark pieces face down on the work table. Using the pattern (diagram 2), trace the outline of four triangular birdhouse roof pieces and cut them out of the bark.

Cutting the Branches

1. Cut four ¾" diameter straight branches, each 10" long for the vertical corner rails A.
2. Cut four ¾" diameter straight branches, each 8" long for the tie beams B at the top of the sides.
3. Cut four ¾" diameter straight branches, each 10" long for the horizontal roof beams C at the roof.
4. Cut four ¾" diameter straight branches, each 8" long for the roof ridge poles D.

Framing the House

1. Place the 4" × 4" pine base on the work table. With the pencil, mark a point at each corner for the ¾" vertical rails A. With pilot holes, nail each corner rail to the base, from the underside (diagram 3).
2. Stand the base (with attached side rails) up. Butt one tie beam B between two corner rails A, at the top. Check for a tight fit; use the garden shears to make any necessary adjustments. Drill pilot holes through the corner rails and nail tie beam B in place.
3. Repeat step 2 with the remaining three tie beams B (diagram 4).

Diagram 2   Roof (cut 4)

Enlarge patterns #1 and #2 by 200%, then take the larger copy and enlarge by a further 200%.

Diagram 3

Diagram 4

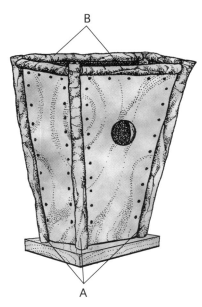

Diagram 5

Adding the Sides

1. Select one bark side and place it behind two corner rails A, and under the tie beam B, with its bottom end flush against the side of the base, making sure it fits properly and trimming if need be.
2. Using the hole punch (or awl), make holes along the top and both sides, approximately ½" in and 2" apart.
3. Repeat steps 1 and 2 with the remaining bark sheets.
4. Join the bark to the framework using vines, by lacing through the holes diagonally over the branch and through the bark.

NOTE: For increased strength, you may choose to lace all the parts together with the needle and heavy thread first, and then add the vine for embellishment.

Making and Adding the Roof

1. Using the hole punch (or awl) punch holes evenly at approximately ½" in, and 1" apart along all four sides of each bark roof section.
2. Arrange and adjust each roof part behind the ridge beams C, and the ridge poles D. Following the directions in step 4 above, lace the sections together.
3. Attach the metal eye bolt to the roof peak with a washer and nut inside the roof (diagram 6).
4. Rest the completed roof structure on top of the house. Mark the four points where the roofing nails will be added. Using the drill and bit, drill pilot holes at these points to join the roof to the tie beams B. Remember to use a drill bit one size smaller than your nail to guarantee a snug fit.

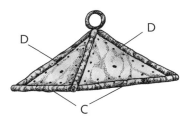

Diagram 6

Diagram 7

Thatched Roof Birdhouse

Hi! My little hut is newly-thatched
I see Blue Morning Glories.

ISSA (1763–1827)

SKILL LEVEL: INTERMEDIATE

THE COZY thatched-roof cottages found nestled in Irish glens are the inspiration for this lift-top, hollow-log model. The hinged top helps to make cleaning easy after each brood has fledged, and the backboard makes it simple to mount along a picket garden fence. Any dry grass can be used for the thatching. This particular roof is made of dried winter fern fronds.

TOOLS

• Single bit axe for felling trees	• Coping saw
• Crosscut hand saw	• Ruler or measuring tape
• Marking pencil	• Carpenter's gouge or woodcarving chisel
• Mallet	• Brace and bit (optional)
• Safety goggles	• Work gloves
• Drill with a selection of bits, including woodboring bit	

MATERIALS

Use a 4" diameter log 9" long for the house. A ¾" thick board, 5½" wide and 25" long, is required for the construction. Seven galvanized box nails, two small butt hinges, and finishing nails are needed to assemble the structure. Light gauge wire (or string) will be required for thatching the roof.

DIRECTIONS

NOTE: The log requires a 2½" cavity for the nesting compartment. One method is to use a power drill and make several large holes in a circular pattern, then further shape the hole with a chisel and mallet. A brace and bit work just as well but take longer. Choose a steel-shanked ratchet brace with a 10" sweep, and an expansion bit that makes a hole 2" across. This method will still require a chisel and mallet to make the cavity ½" larger in diameter.

1. Stand the 4" diameter, 9" long log on the work table. Draw a 2½" diameter circle on the top of the log.
2. Using one of the methods mentioned above, bore a 2½" diameter hole lengthwise completely through the log.
3. Make a pencil mark 2" down from the top of the log. Drill a 1" opening through the log for the entrance hole.
4. Place the 5½" × 25" × ¾" board on the workbench. Cut one piece 13" long for the backboard A; one piece 6" long for the base B; and one piece 6" long for the roof C.
5. Butt base B against backboard A. Using pilot holes, nail the backboard to the base (diagram 1).

6. Place the hollow 9" tall log on the workbench. It is necessary to cut the top of the log at a slant, making the front of the house 1" shorter than the back. Make a mark 8" from the bottom on the front of the house. Using a hand saw, cut the log at a slant, from the top of the 9" back to the 8" front mark. This permits the roof to be attached at an angle.
7. Center the hollow log house on the base B with the entrance hole facing out. Using pilot holes, nail the log house to the base from the underside using galvanized box nails.
8. Rest the roof section along the top of the log and mark out a bevel where the roof meets the backboard (diagram 2). Plane or saw bevel on the roof piece. Install the butt hinges along the bevel of roof section C, and the adjacent backboard A (diagram 3). Test to make sure it flips open properly. If there are gaps between the roof and the hollow log, these will be ideal for ventilation.

The house is now tenant-worthy.

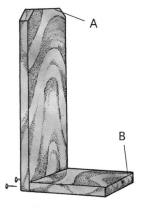

Diagram 1

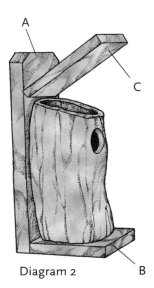

Diagram 2

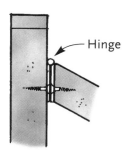

Diagram 3

Thatching the Roof

Covering the roof is fun and adds a different dimension to the structure. Learning to thatch a small area is easy, and the technique can be applied to various other projects. Any dry grass, straw, hay, rye, oats, dry weed, or wildflower may be used for thatching. Fern fronds are gathered during late autumn or winter, when their naturally dry brown stalks are easy to locate in patches along streams and creek beds. To dry ripe green grasses, gather them in the spring or summer. Hang them in bunches, or spread them to dry in a cool place. For a bleached effect, dry them in full sun. To prevent mildew, store any dried material in a cool, airy location, free of moisture.

Thatching consists of tying bundles of dried material together, stapling them in place on the roof, then adding shorter and shorter rows of bundles over the stalks until the whole roof is covered.

Begin by tying three bundles together as shown in diagram 4. Tie them to each other loosely so they will lie side by side when stapled to the roof. Trim the stalks so the bundles are a bit more than 6" long. Staple them in place with the ends of the stalks butted to the backboard (diagram 5).

Tie two 4" long bundles together and staple them over the spaces between the first three (diagram 6).

Finally, tie three or four 2" long bundles together and staple them next to the backboard, covering the stalks of the second layer. The three layers should have a sort of "shingled" look like thatch does (diagram 6).

Diagram 4

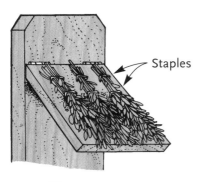

Staples

Diagram 5

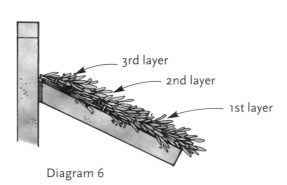

3rd layer

2nd layer

1st layer

Diagram 6

The Finch House

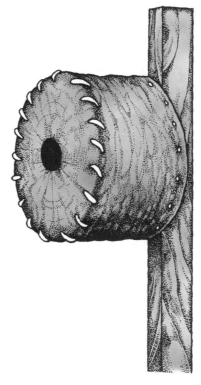

The goldfinch on a thistle-head
Stood scattering seedlets as she fed…

J. INGELOW

CHECK THE FOREST FLOOR for sheets of naturally peeled bark for this design. The house finch requires a 7" deep nesting compartment, but a smaller bird like a chickadee should have a compartment 4" deep. By using this same basic design and altering the depth, you will be able to make a variety of houses.

• Clippers or garden shears	• Ruler or measuring tape
• Marking pencil	• Scissors
• Sharp pocket knife (optional)	• Leather hole punch or awl
• Tack hammer	• Heavy thread and large-eye needle
• Spring-type clothespins for temporary holding	• Work gloves

MATERIALS

You will need one oval wood back, 6" × 10" and ½" thick, a selection of bark sheets; the house sheet is 7" × 29" , and the front is 7" × 10½". Locating exact size sheets is ideal; smaller sheets may be pieced together, however, and will work just as well. You will also need a selection of willow shoots or other pliable branches 33" to 40" long and ⅛" to ¼" in diameter for the inside rim. Vine strips are required for lacing, and ¾" carpet tacks are used to attach the bark to the oval wood back. A dab of glue will be needed to join the bark sheets where they overlap.

DIRECTIONS

Building the Birdhouse

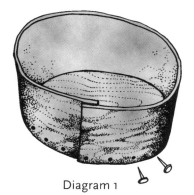

Diagram 1

1. Place the flattened bark pieces on the work table. Using scissors, cut a 7" wide bark sheet 29" long, or cut enough pieces to obtain the correct measurement to surround the outside rim of the 6" × 10" oval wood back.

2. Center one or more bark sheets along the outside rim of the 6" × 10" oval wooden back. Using carpet tacks, fasten the bark to the back at evenly spaced intervals.

3. If more than one sheet is needed, overlap the bark sheets and seal the edges with glue. Continue to tack the sheets to the bottom, at evenly spaced intervals, until the bottom is encircled (diagram 1).

Adding the Top Rim

1. Using the hole punch (or awl), make holes along the top rim of the bark sheet ½" in from the top and approximately 2" apart.
2. Carefully bend one pliable willow shoot into an oval and fit it inside the bark rim. Clamp the willow shoot to the bark with clothespins to hold it in place until the sewing is completed.
3. Join the oval willow shoot to the bark rim using heavy thread and a needle, by sewing through the holes diagonally over the willow shoot and through the bark (diagram 2). Knot the ends of the thread, and remove the clothespins.

Diagram 2

Adding the House Front

1. Cut one bark sheet for the front into an oval approximately 7" × 10½", adjusting it to fit along the outside circumference of the house.
2. Mark a center point on the bark oval; using scissors (or a sharp knife) cut a 1½" diameter hole for the entrance.
3. Join the house front to the sides using vine, by diagonally lacing through holes. If vines are unavailable, use heavy-duty thread.

Place the entrance hole away from the prevailing winds, and attach the birdhouse to a post 8 ft. to 12 ft. above the ground. Do this by driving a common nail through a pre-drilled pilot hole in the center of the back into a post via the entrance hole. Use a steel rod or bolt to drive the nail home (diagram 3).

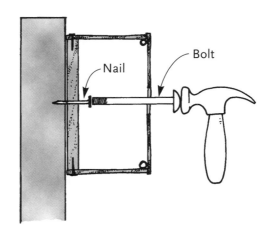

Diagram 3   Attach back board to fence post or yardstake 8–12 ft. above the ground

Robin's Nesting House

Little Bob Robin,
Where do you live?
Up in yonder wood, sir,
On a hazel twig.

NURSERY RHYME

THIS NESTING ROOST is perfect for the garden area and probably will attract other roosting birds, such as swallows, phoebes, and mourning doves. The first signs of spring make us think of turning the soil, sowing seeds, digging in the dirt and, of course, the robin redbreast. Put up one of these houses, and leave it up all year, and you can welcome the robin back every spring as harbinger of a new growing season.

CUTTING CHART

NAME OF PART	QUANTITY	DIAMETER (INCHES)	LENGTH (INCHES)	DESCRIPTION
Floor A	1	8-wide	9½	½" pine or fir
Sides B	2	7-wide	8	½" thick slab wood
Back C	1	11-wide	11	½" thick slab wood
Ridge pole D	1	¾	12	straight stick
Roof E	2	10-wide	11	1" thick slab wood
Front brace F	1	1	11	straight stick split in half

TOOLS

• Single bit axe for felling trees	• Crosscut hand saw
• Saber saw (optional)	• Ruler or measuring tape
• Marking pencil	• Hammer and nails
• Drill with a selection of bits	• Safety goggles
• Work gloves	

MATERIALS

Use any wood boards for the back and sides such as cedar, fir, or maple for the nesting house which measures 8" wide, 11" high, and 7" deep. Its roof is constructed of two wood slabs, each 10" × 11". The exaggerated overhang provides additional protection. One ¾" diameter stick, 12" long is required as a ridge pole; and one 1" diameter branch, 11" long for a rail in front. The 8" × 9" floor is constructed of ½" pine or fir. Galvanized common box nails are used for the joinery.

DIRECTIONS

Cutting the Parts

1. Cut the 8" × 9½" floor A, out of ½" pine.
2. Cut two sides B, each 6" wide and 8" high, out of ½" thick slab wood.
3. Mark a center line on the 11" × 11" wood back C. Make a mark along both outside edges at approximately 5" down from the top. Cut the peaked

shape from the top of the center line, at a slant, down to the 5" mark, thereby forming the peak for the back, C.

4. Cut one ¾" diameter branch for the ridge pole D, 1 ft. long.
5. Cut two roof parts E, each 10" wide and 11" long, out of 1" thick slab wood.
6. Cut one 1" diameter branch for the front brace F, 11" long. Cut this branch in half lengthwise.

Assembling the House

1. With the bark side out, arrange one side along the outside edge of the 8" × 9½" pine floor, and flush with the front edge. Drill pilot holes from the bottom of the floor and into the side. Secure with galvanized common nails.
2. Repeat with the remaining side (diagram 1).
3. With the bark side out, arrange the back in place. NOTE: At this point, it is likely that the floor extends beyond the sides. Using pilot holes, nail the back to the floor from the underside and also nail the back to the sides (diagram 2).
4. With the bark side out, nail the split 11" long front brace F, along the edge of the floor (diagram 2).

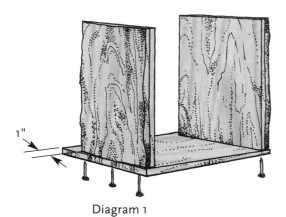

Diagram 1

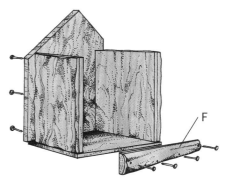

Diagram 2

Adding the Roof

1. Slant one of the roof pieces E over the back and side with the bark side out, allowing the roof to overlap the front approximately 1". Drill two holes each through the roof into the back and into the side B, and nail in place.
2. Repeat to attach the second half of the roof.
3. Place the ¾" ridge pole in the space between the two roof parts. Drill a hole, at each end, through the ridge pole into the roof and nail in place (diagram 3).

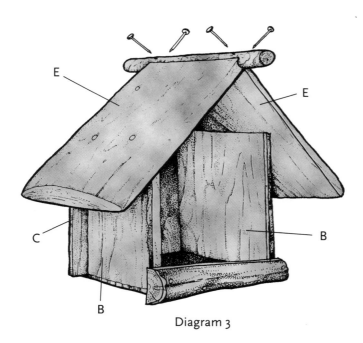

Diagram 3

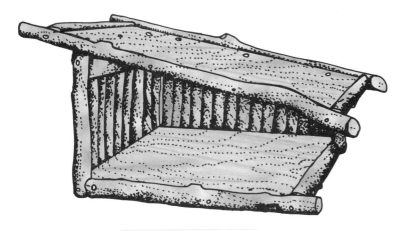

Stockade Shelter

There's hardly a way you can have so much fun
As being outdoors with the brooks as they run,
With the birds as they fly, and the stars as they shine...

JAMES G. NEEDHAM

ATTRACTING BIRDS to your yard can provide hours of entertainment, along with a better understanding of environmental issues and wildlife conservation. Like the Robin's Nesting House on page 140, this open housing project provides a solid foundation for the nests of roosting birds such as robins and flycatchers. An attractive rustic design, constructed of ¾" pine and straight willow branches, encourages tenants to move in. If you clean out the nestbox after the fledglings have left, future generations will return year after year.

CUTTING CHART

NAME OF PART	QUANTITY	DIAMETER (INCHES)	LENGTH (INCHES)	DESCRIPTION
Floor A	1	7-wide	8	½" pine
Roof B	1–2	Total 8½-wide	10	½" pine
Side C	14	½	9	straight
Back D	13	½	5½–9	straight
Trim E	6	½	5½–12	straight

TOOLS

- Crosscut hand saw
- Ruler or measuring tape
- Hammer and nails
- Safety goggles
- Garden clippers
- Marking pencil
- Drill with a selection of bits
- Work gloves

MATERIALS

For the roof use any ½" wood (preferably pine) that measures 8½" × 10", and for the floor use a ½" piece that measures 7" × 8". Gather enough straight willow twigs, 6" to 12" long for the two walls of the house and the trim. NOTE: You will need twelve or thirteen 9" long straight twigs for the side of the shelter, and twelve to fourteen twigs 5½" to 9" long for the back. Use two strips of ½" thick wood, 7" and 7½" long and 1½" wide, for bracing the walls under the roof, and galvanized flathead nails for the joinery.

DIRECTIONS

Assembling the Shelter

1. Nail a 9" long branch corner post to the 7" × 8" floorboard at the front left corner, using a pilot hole (diagram 1).
2. Nail a 5½" long branch corner post to the floorboard at the rear right corner, using a pilot hole (diagram 1).

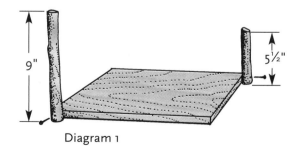

Diagram 1

3. Nail as many 9" long branches to the 7" long strip of wood as will fit (as shown in diagram 2) using pilot holes. Also drill a pilot hole in each twig ¼" up from the bottom end.

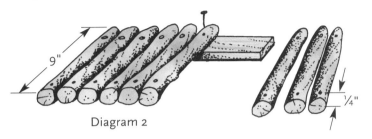

9"

¼"

Diagram 2

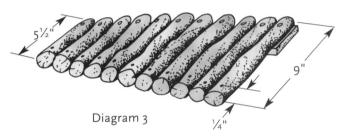

5½"

9"

¼"

Diagram 3

4. Nail as many branches in graduating lengths from 5½" to 9" to the 7½" long wood strip as will fit. NOTE: They must be perpendicular to the bottom, slanting at the top (diagram 3). Drill a pilot hole in each branch ¼" up from the bottom end.

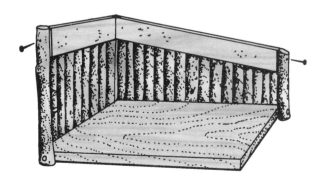

Diagram 4

5. Nail the panel of 9" long branches to the left side of the floorboard with the end of the wood strip butted against the corner post. Drill a hole at the top of the corner post, then nail the post to the end of the strip of wood (diagram 4).

6. Nail the panel of graduated branches to the back of the floorboard, butting the wood strip against the wood strip on the side panel. Using a pilot hole, nail these strips together.

7. Nail the top of the right rear corner post to the end of the wood strip on the back panel as was done with the other corner post (diagram 4).

Adding the Roof

1. Lay the 8½" × 10" roof board on the two walls of branches so it overhangs the open side by at least 1" (diagram 5).

2. Drill three holes through the roof into the tops of three of the side branches and repeat with the back branches.

3. Nail the roof board into the tops of the branches.

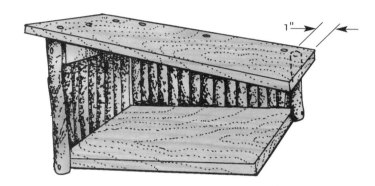

Diagram 5

Adding the Roof and Floor Trim

1. Using pilot holes, nail an 8½" long branch onto the edge of both sides of the roof as trim.

2. Trim the front and back edges of the roof with 12" long branches nailed in place using pilot holes.

3. Using pilot holes, nail a 6½" long branch to the edge of the open side of the floor (the right side) to trim it.

4. Finally, nail an 8" long branch to the front edge of the floorboard.

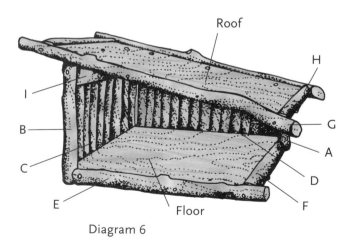

Diagram 6

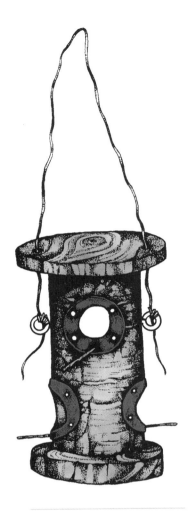

Birch & Copper Feeder

I have often wondered
if any one was so indifferent to birds
that he would not turn his head
if a Cardinal flashed by.

CHARLES CONRAD ABBOTT, 1895

SKILL LEVEL: INTERMEDIATE

THE TOP LIFTS OFF this white birch feeder to allow for easy refilling, while the copper plates surrounding the openings prevent larger birds or animals from enlarging them. This design with its four openings invites several guests to dine at the same time.

TOOLS

• Single bit axe for felling trees, if you don't have a wood pile	• Crosscut hand saw
• Brace and bit	• Sandpaper
• Ruler or measuring tape	• Marking pencil
• Drill and a selection of bits, including an expansion bit	• Tin snips
• Carpenter's compass	• Phillips-head screwdriver
• Safety goggles	• Work gloves

MATERIALS

Use a white birch log, 9" to 10" long and 4" to 5" in diameter, or other hardwoods such as beech, hickory, or maple for the feeder. You will need two 6" to 7" diameter wood slices, 1"–1½" thick for the base and roof. A sheet of copper, 6" × 24" will be required, along with sixteen ½" round head Phillips-head screws, and two screw-eyes. Four ⅛" diameter twigs, 3" long are used for perches, and twine or rawhide for hanging.

DIRECTIONS
Building the Feeder

1. The feeder requires a 3" to 4" diameter cavity for the feeding compartment. With luck, a wood pile, or walk in the woods will offer a partially hollow log. If you have to bore out the center of the log, stand the 9" to 10" long, 4" to 5" diameter log on the workbench. Draw a 3" to 4" diameter circle on the top of the log. Using a power drill, or brace and bit, bore a 3" to 4" diameter hole completely through the log.
2. Center a pencil mark approximately 2½" down from the top of the log on the front and on the back of the log. Drill a 1" opening on each side.

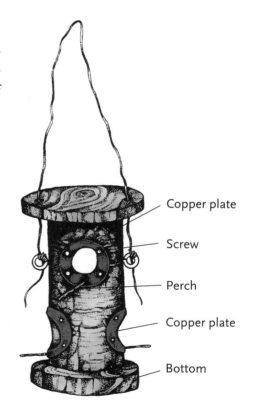

Diagram 1

Copper plate

Screw

Perch

Copper plate

Bottom

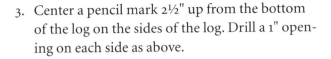

3. Center a pencil mark 2½" up from the bottom of the log on the sides of the log. Drill a 1" opening on each side as above.

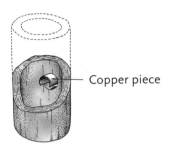

Diagram 2   Inside view showing copper opening cover (NOTE: These are placed over every opening).

Adding Copper Disks and Shields

1. Using a carpenter's compass and tin snips, draw and cut out four copper disks 3" to 3½" in diameter. Using the compass, draw a 1" circle on the center of a copper disk, and using the tin snips cut out the opening. Repeat with the remaining three copper disks.

2. Arrange a disk over the 1" opening. Using the drill and bit, drill five holes through the disk and the log, as shown in the copper disk diagram 3. Attach disk to log with four Phillips-head screws. Glue the twig perch into the remaining hole.

3. Repeat with the remaining three copper disks.

4. Cut four pieces of sheet copper approximately 2" × 2". Bend and fit along the upper section of each 1" opening, as illustrated in diagram 2.

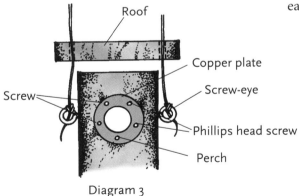

Roof
Copper plate
Screw-eye
Screw
Phillips head screw
Perch

Diagram 3

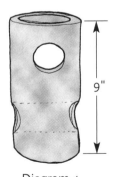

9"

Diagram 4

Final Assembly

1. Place the feeder on the workbench, bottom side up. Center one 6" to 7" diameter log slice, 2" thick (the bottom) on the feeder bottom. Using pilot holes, nail the bottom to the feeder with two galvanized nails from the underside.
2. Screw a screw-eye into either side of the feeder, approximately 3" down from the top.
3. Drill two ¼" diameter holes through the log slice top as shown in diagram 3. Place the top on the feeder, and hold in place by threading twine through the holes down to the screw-eyes where it is tied off.

To fill, lift off the top and pour in bird seed. Hang outdoors from a tree limb or post.

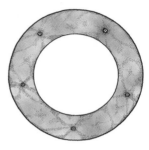

Diagram 3

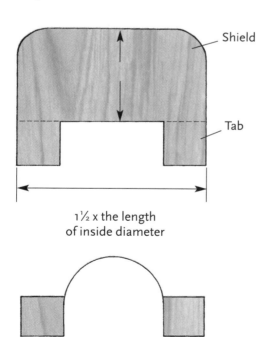

Shield

Tab

1½ x the length
of inside diameter

Diagram 6 Tabs bent back to
the outside of feeder

Grapevine Roof Feeder

I value my garden more for being full of blackbirds than of cherries, and very frankly give them fruit for their song.

JOSEPH ADDISON

AN AFTERNOON is all it will take to build this bird feeder. Gathering materials is simple because any kind of twigs will do. This easy-to-make feeder is great fun to build, and very rewarding when you observe the birds feeding at the generously sized tray. Hang from a tree with heavy cord.

MATERIALS

You will need a selection of 1" diameter hardwood twigs, including two forked twigs, ranging in length from 8" to 1 ft. An 8½" × 1 ft. piece of ½" thick

C U T T I N G   C H A R T

NAME OF PART	QUANTITY	DIAMETER (INCHES)	LENGTH (INCHES)	DESCRIPTION
Tray ends A	2	1	8½	straight
Tray sides B	2	1	14	straight
Roof supports C	4	1	8	straight
Roof peaks D	2	1	16–20	*forked
Roof side brace E	2	1	11	straight
Ridge pole F	1	1	11	straight
Tray	1	8½	12	½" scrap lumber

*Forks form the peaks, therefore select branches that can be trimmed at both ends of the fork. The ridge pole will be installed, at the forks, between the two roof peak braces D.

T O O L S

• Single bit axe for felling trees	• Crosscut hand saw
• Ruler or measuring tape	• Marking pencil
• Clippers or garden shears	• Drill and a selection of bits
• Hammer and galvanized nails	• Safety goggles
• Work gloves	

plywood is required for the tray. Gather enough vines to weave the top (any local vine, such as grapevine, Virginia creeper, bittersweet, wisteria, or kudzu). 1½" galvanized common nails, 1" finishing nails, and a length of heavy cord 20" long for hanging are also needed.

DIRECTIONS
Cutting the Branches
1. Cut two 1" diameter branches, 8½" long for the tray ends A.
2. Cut two 1" diameter branches, 12" long for the tray sides B.
3. Cut four 1" diameter branches, 8" long for the roof supports C.
4. Cut two forked 1" diameter branches, 16" to 20" long for the roof peak braces D.
5. Cut two 1" diameter branches, 11" long for the roof side braces E.

6. Cut one straight 1" diameter branch, 11" long for the ridge pole F.
7. Cut a piece of ½" pine, 8½" × 12" for the feeder tray.
8. Approximately 25 pieces of supple vines, 15" to 20" long are required for weaving the roof.

Drilling the Pilot Holes and Assembling the Tray
Make the pilot holes snug; the hole should be ⅜" to ½" shorter than the nail is long.

1. Lay one tray end A against the 8½" edge of the plywood feeder tray. Using a ⅛" bit, drill pilot holes, and attach tray end A to the plywood with galvanized nails.
2. Repeat step 1 to attach the remaining tray end A.
3. Using the same method, attach the tray sides B to the 14" sides of the feeder tray, drilling pilot holes and nailing in place with the galvanized nails (diagram 1).

Adding the Roof Supports
NOTE: The roof supports are installed at a slant.
Mark the locations of the four roof supports 1" from each side (diagram 2), and drill pilot holes at a slant through the plywood (diagram 3). Also drill into the end of each roof support (diagram 4). Nail each roof support in place from the underside of the plywood tray (diagram 5). NOTE: Trim roof supports C so they are slightly angled at the base.

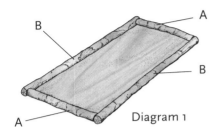

Diagram 1

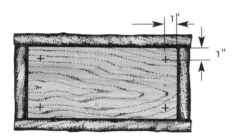

Diagram 2

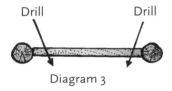

Diagram 3

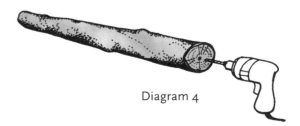

Diagram 4

Adding the Roof

1. Drill pilot holes through the two forked roof peaks into the ends of the ridge pole F and two roof side braces E. Nail these five pieces together with galvanized common nails (diagram 6).

2. Center the forked roof peaks over the four roof supports allowing 2" to 4" to overhang at each side to help keep the seed dry. Drill pilot holes down through the roof peaks into the ends of the roof supports and nail in place with galvanized common nails.

3. Weave the vines under and over the side roof braces E, and the ridge pole F, filling in tightly. Check your progress as you go along and push each row of weaving close together to ensure a tight roof.

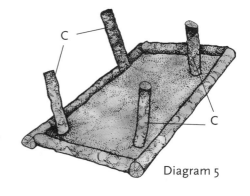

Diagram 5

To hang the bird feeder, tie a 20" length of rope or wire around both roof side braces. For another hanging option, drill a hole through the ridge pole at the center, screw in a screw-eye, and tie the wire or rope through the screw-eye.

Diagram 6

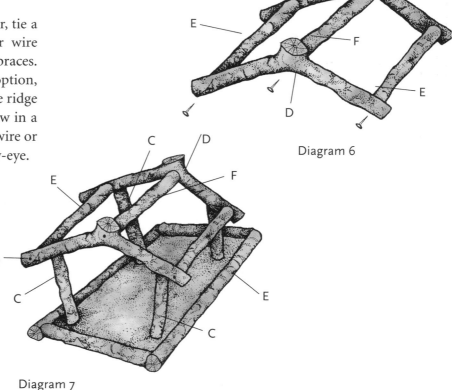

Diagram 7

Suet Feeder

*The north wind doth blow,
and we shall have snow.*

MOTHER GOOSE

SKILL LEVEL: BEGINNER

THIS SIMPLE PROJECT is a great way for beginners to get started. Hanging in your winter garden and filled with Bird Seed Pudding, this feeder will attract chickadees, nuthatches, and winter cardinals. To make old-fashioned Bird Seed Pudding: Mix ¼ cup melted suet with ¾ cup bird seed (including peanuts, millet, and sunflower seeds); press into feeder openings, and place in a cool place or refrigerator to set. Hang it outside for your wildlife friends.

• Crosscut hand saw	• Ruler or measuring tape
• Marking pencil	• Vise
• Electric drill with a selection of bits	• Wood glue (optional)
• Work gloves	• Safety goggles
• Galvanized metal screw-eye and rope, or leather lace for hanging	

MATERIALS

Choose a hardwood such as white birch, beech, or hickory. The suet feeder requires a branch 1 ft. long and 2" to 3" in diameter. Eight twigs, approximately 3" long and ¼" to ½" in diameter, will be needed for the perches.

DIRECTIONS

1. Cut off all protrusions from a 1 ft. long branch, and sand the surface smooth if necessary. All perch holes are approximately 1" below the suet holes.
2. Using the diagram (right) as a guide, measure and mark the locations where the holes are to be drilled.
3. Place the branch firmly in a vise. (Wrap the branch with soft fabric such as terry cloth, to avoid crushing it in the vise while you are working with it.) Drill 1" diameter holes for the suet openings, and ¼" diameter holes for the perch. The suet holes may be drilled completely through the branch. The holes for the perches need only be 1" deep. Use a dab of wood glue in each perch hole.
4. Add the galvanized metal screw-eye to the top of the branch and tie a heavy cord to it for hanging.

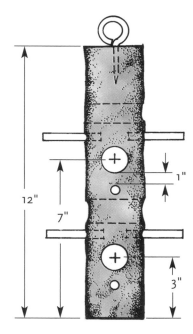

Diagram 1

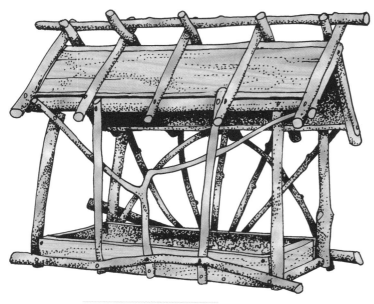

Cabin Bird Feeder

One winter in December, a solitary red-breasted nuthatch
took up his abode with me, attracted by the suet and nuts
I had placed on a maple-tree-trunk in front of my study window…

JOHN BURROUGHS
"THE SPRING BIRD PROCESSION"

THIS CABIN is for the birds and they will love it. The generous-sized feeding tray guarantees a bountiful banquet, while the pitched roof provides a sheltered and cozy spot. Whether you hang it from a tree with a rope, or install it on a post, this rustic bird feeder will be a big hit. Directions are given for the basic size and shape, and you are encouraged to add your own touches with some decorative embellishments. A myriad of twig patterns can trim the feeder; just make sure the birds can reach the feed. The scrap lumber roof can be painted, stained, or left to weather naturally.

CUTTING CHART

NAME OF PART	QUANTITY	DIAMETER (INCHES)	LENGTH (INCHES)	DESCRIPTION
Corner posts A	4	¾	8	straight
Roof supports B	2	½	16	straight
Roof peaks C	10	½	8–9	straight
Ridge pole D	1	¼	19	straight
Roof trim E	4	½	5–6	straight
Tray end trim F	2	½–¾	6–7	*hardwood
Tray side trim G	2	½–¾	16	*hardwood
Decorative trim H	8–15	¼–½	7–10	*hardwood

*NOTE: The hardwood trim branches can be straight, forked, or pliable.

TOOLS

- Crosscut hand saw
- Clippers or garden shears
- Marking pencil
- Hammer and nails
- Work gloves
- Coping saw or miter box
- Ruler or measuring tape
- Drill and a selection of bits
- Safety goggles

MATERIALS

You will need a selection of ¼" to ¾" diameter hardwood twigs, ranging in length from 8" to 17". Use a 7" × 11" piece of scrap wood for the tray; two pieces of 6" × 15" scrap wood for the roof; and two 7" long, and two 12" long pieces of ½" wood for the tray ends and tray sides. Use galvanized 1½" nails and 1" finishing nails for the joinery.

DIRECTIONS

Cutting the Branches

1. Cut four ¾" diameter branches, 8" long for the corner posts A.
2. Cut two ½" diameter branches, 16" long for the roof supports B.
3. Cut ten ½" diameter branches, 8" to 9" long for the roof peaks C.
4. Cut one ¼" diameter branch, 19" long for the ridge pole D.

5. Cut four ½" diameter branches, 5" to 6" long for the roof trim E.
6. Cut two ½" to ¾" diameter branches, 6" to 7" long for the tray end trim F.
7. Cut two ½" to ¾" diameter branches, 16" long for the tray side trim G.
8. Cut a dozen or more ¼" to ½" diameter branches, 7" to 12" long for the decorative trim H.
9. Cut a piece of ½" pine, 7" × 11" for the feeder tray.
10. Cut two pieces of ¼" pine, 7" long for the tray ends.
11. Cut two pieces of ¼" pine, 12" long for the tray sides.

Drilling the Pilot Holes and Assembling the Tray

Make sure the pilot holes are snug; the hole should be smaller and ⅜" to ½" shallower than the nail is long.

1. To form the tray, butt one tray end against the 7" long side of the feeder tray. Using a ⅛" diameter bit, drill pilot holes, and attach the tray end to the feeder tray using galvanized roofing nails.
2. Repeat step 1 to attach the remaining tray end.
3. Using the same method, affix the tray sides to the 12" side of the feeder tray, drilling pilot holes and nailing in place with galvanized roofing nails.

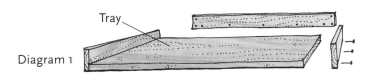

Tray

Diagram 1

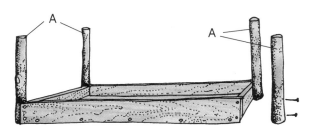

A

A

Diagram 2

Adding the Corner Post

1. Turn the tray on its side and arrange one corner post A on one outside corner of the feeder tray. Mark the location and drill a pilot hole and nail in place.
2. Repeat to attach the remaining three corner posts.

Adding the Roof

1. Using pilot holes, nail one roof support B, into the top ends of the two corner posts along the 12" side of the feeder tray.
2. Repeat with the remaining roof support (diagram 3).
3. Butt the long edges of the roof sections against each other so it forms a right angle. Drill four holes through both roof sections, and nail in place (diagram 4).
4. Place the roof supports then drill pilot holes, and nail in place.
5. Arrange the ten roof rafters C upon the roof, five rafters to each side. Allow them to overhang the roof supports B by approximately 1½" and to cross each other at the top. Drill a hole at each end of the roof peak, through the roof supports B and the roof, and nail in place (diagram 5).
6. Place the 19" long ridge pole along the crossed rafters and nail it in place.
7. Referring to diagram 6 and using a coping saw or miter box, bevel one end of roof trim E, to form the peak. Repeat with the remaining three roof trims.
8. Arrange the roof trim so mitered ends meet and nail it to the roof edge.

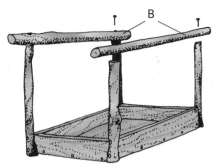

Diagram 3

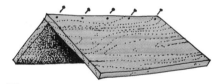

Diagram 4

Adding Decorative Trim

1. Refer to diagram 6 and arrange tray end trim in place along the front of the feeding tray. Drill and nail in place. Repeat with remaining tray end trim F.
2. Refer to the picture for decorative trim place-

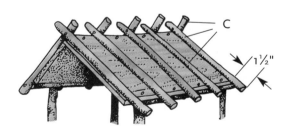

Diagram 5

ment. To form the spoke trim, arrange five ¼" diameter straight branches against the tray sides and the roof support B, and drill and nail in place using thin finishing nails.

3. To form the arch, gently bend one ¼" diameter, 22" long pliable twig, and using the same method as above, nail it in place.

4. Add side trim G over decorative trim, as pictured in diagram 6.

5. Continue adding trim as you wish to make your feeder an original.

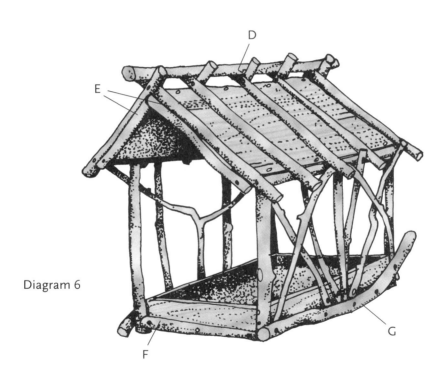

Diagram 6

CHAPTER 6

Furniture

The Willy Loveseat

Great pleasure was it to be there
Till green turned duskier and the moon
Coloured the corn-sheaves like gold hair.

ALGERNON CHARLES SWINBURNE

A WILLOWER or person who works with willow was called a Willy in the Scottish Highlands and Northern English villages in the eighteenth century; therefore this classically designed loveseat is named The Willy. With its sturdy stretchers and high back it is perfectly at home on a porch, by poolside, or in a garden. This practical piece, built in a weekend, is sure to be enjoyed for many years.

CUTTING CHART

NAME OF PART	QUANTITY	DIAMETER (INCHES)	LENGTH (INCHES)	DESCRIPTION
Back legs A	2	1½	36	hardwood
Front legs B	2	1½	25	hardwood
Arms C	2	1½	17	hardwood
Leg spreaders D	5	1¾	32	hardwood
Front/back diagonal braces E	4	1–1¼	21	hardwood
Seat/back F	3	1–1¼	13	hardwood
Top rail G	1	¾	37	peaked, hardwood
Top trim H	8	½	1–21	hardwood
Side spreaders I	4	1–1¼	15–16	hardwood
Side diagonal braces J	4	1	18	hardwood
Seat branches L	16	¾–1	36	hardwood
Arch trim	4–8	½	25–30	pliable willow branches

TOOLS

- Crosscut hand saw
- Garden shears or clippers
- Measuring tape
- Hammer
- Work gloves

- Single bit axe for felling trees
- ⅜" variable-speed drill
- Marking pencil
- Safety goggles

MATERIALS

Willow, hickory, birch, beech, or any hardwood branches ranging in length from 13" to 3 ft. and from ¾" to 1¾" in diameter may be used for the basic structure. You will also need sixteen ¾" to 1" diameter branches, 3 ft. long for the seat, along with a few pliable willow shoots for the back trim, and a peak-shaped branch 37" long for the top rail. Galvanized common nails in assorted sizes (#4p, #6p, #8p, and #10p) and about three dozen 1" finishing nails are also required. You will need a 10" length of ⅛" diameter steel rod (such as "Drill-Rod") for threading the top trim.

DIRECTIONS

Cutting the Branches

1. Cut two 1½" diameter branches for the back legs A, each 3 ft. long.
2. Cut two 1½" diameter branches for the front legs B, each 25" long.
3. Cut two 1½" diameter branches for the arms C, each 17" long.
4. Cut five 1¾" diameter branches for the leg spreaders D, each 32" long.
5. Cut four 1" to 1¼" diameter branches for the front/back diagonal braces E, each 21" long.
6. Cut three 1" to 1¼" diameter branches for the seat back F, each 13" long.
7. Cut one ¾" diameter peaked (bent or arched) branch 37" long for the top rail G.
8. Cut eight ½" diameter branches in graduated sizes from 1" to 21" for the top trim H.
9. Cut seven 1" to 1¼" diameter branches for the side spreaders I, each 16" long.
10. Cut four 1" diameter branches for the side diagonal braces J, each 18" long.

Laying Out the Sub-Assembly

1. Butt one spreader D between both back legs A, 3" up from the bottom of each leg. Using a pilot hole, nail in place from the outside of each leg.
2. Butt one spreader D between both back legs A, 13" up from the bottom beam. Nail in place as in step 1 above.
3. Butt one spreader D between both back legs A, 5" from the top of the legs. Nail in place as before (diagram 1).
4. Butt one seat/back F between the two top back beams D, at the center (16" from either end). Drill holes from the top and bottom of the beams, and nail the seat back F in place.
5. Arrange the remaining seat/backs F at approximately 8" on either side of the center seat/back. Using pilot holes, nail in place (diagram 1).

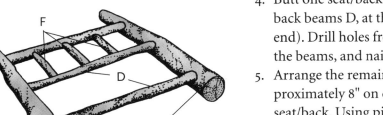

Diagram 1   Back leg assembly

6. Butt one spreader D between both front legs B, 3" up from the bottom of each leg. Nail in place as in step 1 above (diagram 2).

7. Butt the remaining spreader D between both front legs B, 13" up from the bottom beam. Using pilot holes, nail in place.

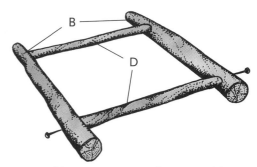

Diagram 2   Front leg assembly

Joining the Back- and Front-Leg Assemblies

1. Butt the top and bottom side spreaders I, between the inside of the front and back legs at the same points as the front and back spreaders D. Drill pilot holes and nail them in place from the outside of the legs.

2. Nail the top and bottom side spreaders on the opposite side, in the same way.

3. Butt one arm C against a back leg A and across a front leg B, allowing it to extend approximately 1". From the top, drill a pilot hole and nail arm C into the top of leg B. With arm C horizontal, drill a pilot hole from the back of the back leg, partway into the end of arm C, and nail in place.

4. Repeat with the opposite arm.

5. Lay the whole assembly on its back (diagram 3). Position one front/back diagonal brace E on the inside of the top spreader D, and along the inside of the back leg, resting it on the top of the side spreader I. Drill and nail diagonal brace E in place through

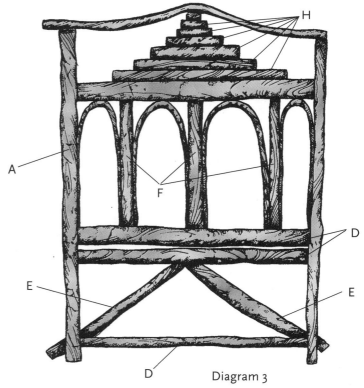

Diagram 3

the brace into the top spreader D and the back leg B.

6.   Repeat with the opposite diagonal brace.

7.   Turn the assembly over onto its front legs and nail two diagonal braces E to the inside of the front legs as described for the back ones.

8.   Add the four side diagonal braces J inside the top side spreaders I, and the inside of the lower back and front spreaders D.

Adding the Seat

1.   With the loveseat standing upright, butt the three remaining side spreaders I between the top front and back spreaders D as seat supports opposite each seat back F (diagram 4). Using pilot holes, nail each part K to the back and front beams.

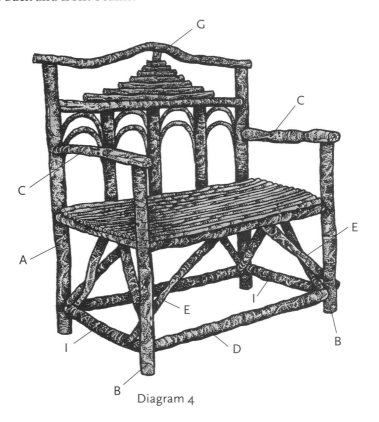

Diagram 4

2. Beginning at the back and working toward the front, position seat branches L along the top of the five side spreaders I. Drill pilot holes and nail the branches in place, forming a tight-fitting seat.

3. Trim the ends of the front seat branch for a tight fit between the two front legs.

Adding the Trim and Top Rail

1. Carefully bend four 25" to 30" lengths of pliable willow branches; form into an arch and nail in place between the seat/back parts F, and the back legs as pictured.

2. Lay the top rail G across the ends of the back legs A. Drill pilot holes and temporarily nail in place to hold its position.

3. Arrange top trim pieces H as pictured. At the center point drill completely through each part, and partway through the top beam D. Insert a 9" or 10" length of ⅛" diameter steel rod in the drilled hole on the top beam D. Thread all top trim parts H on the inserted wire (diagram 5).

Diagram 5

4. Drill a hole partway through the top rail G under the center peak. Arrange the center peak in place on the wire, trimming the wire with a hacksaw if necessary. Drill pilot holes and nail in place.

A handsome piece of furniture, complete in itself, The Willy Loveseat is surprisingly comfortable—it is built to help you enjoy the view. Add a few cozy calico or cotton duck pillows if you are using it in a covered area. The slight color variations of the wood seem to improve with time when the piece is left in its natural state. If, however, you choose to paint it, consider using a distinctive shade of green such as sage or bayberry to complement your outdoor area.

Cedar & Vine Garden Bench

When I discovered a new plant, I sat down beside it for a minute or a day, to make its acquaintance and hear what it had to tell…

JOHN MUIR

I DECIDED TO MAKE this bench when a mass of Virginia creeper vine was cut to make way for a new pond on a neighbor's property. I hated to see such a mother lode go to waste, and enlisted help to wrap, twist, and fasten the flexible vine on the garden bench before it dried. The materials dictated the design, and I hope it will inspire your rustic imagination.

C U T T I N G   C H A R T

NAME OF PART	QUANTITY	DIAMETER (INCHES)	LENGTH (INCHES)	DESCRIPTION
Back legs A	2	2	33–36	pliable, hardwood
Front leg B	1	2	30	pliable, hardwood
Curved front leg B1	1	2	34	pliable, hardwood
Top side beams C	2	1½	21	hardwood
Bottom side spreaders D	2	1½	23	hardwood
Arm E	1	1½	27	hardwood
Arm/back wrap E1	1	1–1½	95	pliable, hardwood
Bottom braces F	3	1¼–1¾	55	pliable, hardwood
Leg-to-leg, or Leg-to-seat brace G	2	¾–1½	20	pliable, hardwood
Seat	1	16	54	1½" thick lumber or (or several pieces totalling 16" width)

T O O L S

- Single bit axe for felling trees
- ⅜" variable-speed drill
- Marking pencil
- Clippers or garden shears
- Work gloves

- Crosscut hand saw
- Measuring tape
- Hammer
- Safety goggles
- Pocket knife (optional)

MATERIALS

Cedar, willow, hickory, or any pliable branches ranging from 20" to 95" in length, and 1½" to 2½" in diameter may be used for the basic structure. A flexible (green) length of vine is used for the wrapped loops; however, a selection of pliable branches, as long as possible and ¼" to ½" in diameter, may be substituted. Two or three 1½" thick boards nailed together may be used for the seat, which is 16" × 54". Galvanized common nails in assorted sizes (#4p, #6p, #8p, #12p, and #16p) and a few handfuls of 1" finishing nails will be required. The following directions are for the basic construction. Design your own back and fill in with available materials.

DIRECTIONS

Cutting the Branches

1. Cut two 2" diameter branches for the back legs A, 33" to 36" long. NOTE: The back legs vary in length because one or both may splay outward during construction. It is better to cut the longer version and trim when necessary.

2. Cut one 2" diameter branch for the front leg B, 30" long.

3. Cut one 2" diameter branch for the curved front leg B1, 34" long, remembering to allow for some trimming that may be required.

4. Cut two 1½" diameter branches for the top side beams C, each 21" long.

5. Cut two 1½" diameter branches for the bottom side spreaders D, each 23" long.

6. Cut one 1½" diameter branch for the arm E, 27" long.

7. Cut one 1" to 1½" diameter flexible branch for the arm/back wrap E1, 95" long.

8. Cut three or more 1¼" to 1¾" diameter pliable branches for the bottom braces F, each 55" long.

9. Cut two ¾" to 1½" diameter pliable branches for the leg-to-seat (or leg-to-leg) braces G, each 20" long.

10. Cut one or more pieces of 1½" thick lumber 54" long and measuring 16" deep.

11. Have an assortment of vine or flexible twigs ready to create the back support.

Laying Out the Basic Construction

1. Overlap side beam C across back leg A and front leg B, 18" to 19" up from the bottom of both legs on the outside. The beam will extend approximately 1" beyond both legs. Join beam C to the legs using #12p nails.

2. Overlap top side beam C across back leg A and curved front leg B1, 18" to 19" up from the bottom of both legs on the outside. The beam will extend approximately 1" beyond both legs. Using pilot holes, nail as in step 1 above.

3. Make a 16" × 54" seat with two or more 1½" thick boards by nailing three two-by-four battens on the underside (diagram 1).

4. Position the seat between both leg/beam assemblies, and with pilot holes through the beams only, nail into the ends of the seat planks from the outside of the beams. Make sure the seat is level at this step. Nail one side first then use a builder's level to assist in nailing the other side.

5. Lay arm E on top of front leg B and its corresponding back leg A. The arms should extend about 2" beyond the front and back of the legs. Make sure the back of the arm is long enough to support the arm/back wrap E1.

6. Drill holes through the arm and into the top of the legs at the point where they meet. Nail in place using #8p or #10p nails.

7. Lay arm/back wrap E1 on top of the curved front leg B1. The arm extends 2" to 3" beyond the curved front leg. Drill a hole through the arm and into the top of the front leg B1 at the point where they meet. Nail in place.

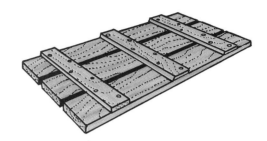

Diagram 1   Underside of seat

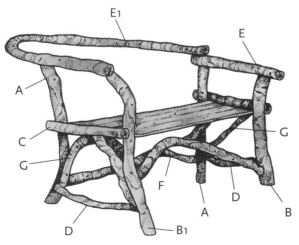

Diagram 2

8. Carefully place arm/back part E1 on top of its corresponding back leg A, and nail in place.

9. Continue to carefully move the extended E1 part into a pleasing shape with its end resting on top of the installed arm E, thus forming the back rest as pictured. Nail E1 to E at the point where they meet.

10. Butt bottom side spreader D between the front and back legs approximately 5" up from the bottom. Nail in place using a #10p, or #12p nail. Repeat with the opposite side.

Bracing and Completing

Diagonal braces strengthen the structure. Add as many as you feel are needed for your design.

1. Butt one bottom brace F between both back legs approximately 7" up from the bottom. Drill and nail in place from the outside.

2. Because the bottom braces F are longer than the length of the bench, the braces will arch upward when placed between the legs and try to spread the legs apart. Lay a second bottom brace F along the inside of both back legs. Drill and nail in place through the second brace F into both back legs.

3. Butt and nail the remaining bottom brace F between both front legs.

4. Nail the remaining 20" braces G from leg to leg, or leg to the underside of the seat as required for added stability.

5. Wrap, weave, loop, and arrange the vines or twigs between the arm/back wrap E1, and the seat to create a sturdy back support. Drill pilot holes and nail in place to E, E1, and the seat, with finishing nails, where needed.

Garden Chair

*The garden is the place I go to
for refuge and shelter,
not the house.*

"ELIZABETH & HER GERMAN GARDEN,"
MAY 16, 1880

GARDEN SEATS, with their decorative value, are appreciated by the gardener who takes the time to sit and think. Add this straightforward chair to your garden scene and stop to enjoy the view.

MATERIALS
You will need hardwood branches such as willow, beech, or birch. Lengths will range from 7" to 3 ft., and diameters from ¾" to 2". You will also need a piece of lumber 3¾" wide × 42" long. Galvanized common nails, and finishing nails in assorted sizes (#4p, #6p, #8p, and #10p) are required.

CUTTING CHART

NAME OF PART	QUANTITY	DIAMETER (INCHES)	LENGTH (INCHES)	DESCRIPTION
Back legs A	2	1¾–2	36	hardwood
Back seat support B	1	1	12	hardwood
Front seat support C	1	1	12	hardwood
Front legs D	2	1¾–2	16	hardwood
Seat boards	3	3¾-wide × 14 long ea.		lumber
Crossed leg braces E	8	¾	13–15	hardwood
Back stretcher F	1	1	7	hardwood
Top beam G	1	1	19	hardwood
End fretwork H	2	1	9	hardwood
Center fretwork I	2	1	9	hardwood
Back legs trim J	1	¾	11	hardwood
Seat trim K	4	1¼	7½–13	split/hardwood

TOOLS

- Single bit axe for felling trees
- Coping saw
- Ruler or measuring tape
- Drill with a selection of bits
- Miter box (optional)
- Work gloves
- Crosscut hand saw
- Clippers
- Marking pencil
- Hammer
- Safety goggles

DIRECTIONS

Cutting the Branches

1. Cut two 1¾" to 2" diameter branches for the back legs A, each 3 ft. long.
2. Cut one 1" diameter branch for the back seat support B, 1 ft. long.
3. Cut one 1" diameter branch for the front seat support C, 1 ft. long.
4. Cut two 1¾" to 2" diameter branches for the front legs D, each 16" long.
5. Cut eight ¾" diameter branches for the front leg braces E, each 13" to 15" long.

6. Cut one 1" diameter branch for the back stretcher F, 7" long.

7. Cut one 1" diameter branch for the top beam G, 19" long.

8. Cut two 1" diameter branches for the end fretwork H, each 9" long.

9. Cut two 1" diameter branches for the center fretwork I, each 9" long.

10. Cut one ¾" diameter branch for the back legs trim J, 11" long.

11. Split two 1¼" diameter branches, and cut 7½" to 13" long for the seat trim K.

12. Cut three ¾" thick and 3¾" wide seat boards 14" long for the seat.

Laying Out the Sub-Assembly

1. Begin construction from the back. Lay out the two back legs A parallel, approximately 8" apart on the workbench. Mark a point 15" from the bottom of both back legs. At the 15" mark lay the back seat support B across both legs (1" to 2" of part B will extend beyond the legs). Drill a pilot hole through part B into part A, and nail in place (diagram 1).

2. Place the two front legs D, parallel and approximately 8" apart on the workbench. Lay the front seat support C across both legs 15" from the bottom of both legs; the seat will rest on top of the front (and the back) seat supports. Nail part C to the front legs D, using pilot holes (diagram 2).

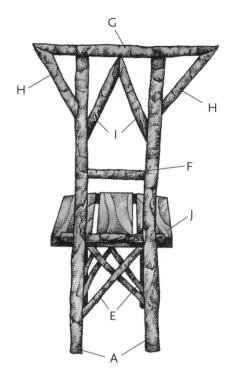

Back view

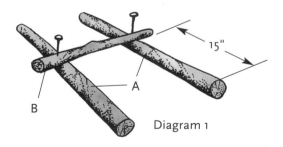

Diagram 1

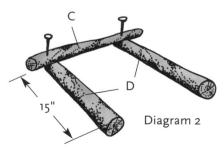

Diagram 2

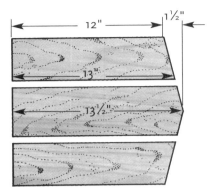

Diagram 3   Seat

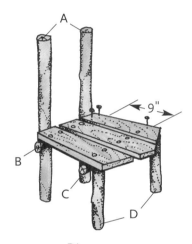

Diagram 4

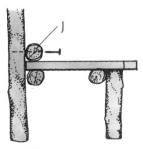

Diagram 5

Making the Seat

Refer to the seat layout in diagram 3. Lay out the overall seat pattern on paper or plywood. Then trim the three boards to match: center the first board over the pattern, then hold the two side boards in place on either side with weights. With a ruler draw the angled front edge across the boards. Cut along these lines.

1. NOTE: The back seat support B and front seat support C face each other inside the chair. Place the center seat board on top of the back seat support B; nail in place from the top of the seat. Make a mark on the board 9" from the back seat support B. At this mark nail the seat board into the front seat support C using pilot holes.

2. Position the side seat boards along the back and front seat supports with the outside edges flush with the ends of seat supports B and C. Drill pilot holes and nail seat boards to front and back seat supports C and B (diagram 4).

3. Butt back stretcher F between the back legs 23" from the bottom. Drill pilot holes and nail in place from the outside of legs A.

4. Place seat beam J across the seat slats, overlapping back legs A. Using pilot holes, nail in place through seat beam J and back legs A (diagram 5).

5. Butt back stretcher F between the back legs 8" above the seat and nail in place with pilot holes.

Adding the Crossed Leg Braces

1. To add the *front-to-back* leg braces E, nail from the inside front leg, 4" from the bottom to the back seat support on both sides.

2. To add the *back-to-front* leg braces E, nail from the inside back leg 4" from the bottom (overlapping the installed cross brace), to a location on the inside of the front leg approximately 1 ft. from the bottom.

3. To add the *back-to-back* leg braces E, nail from the inside of one back leg, 4" from the bottom to the outside of the opposite back leg. This will be at a location close to where the seat meets the back legs. Repeat with an additional crossed brace, overlapping the first.

4. To add the *front-to-front* leg braces E, attach one crossed leg brace E from the front of the front seat support C, to a front leg A, approximately 2" to 3" from the bottom of the leg. Repeat with the last remaining leg brace, overlapping the first.

Adding the Fretwork and Seat Trim

1. Position top beam G, across the top of the back legs A. Drill through both pieces and nail in place through the top of part G into the ends of back legs A.

2. Refer to diagram 1, and arrange the end fretwork pieces H, beveling the ends with the coping saw. NOTE: Using a miter box helps to cut the angle to join the parts.

3. Refer again to diagram 1 and lay out the end fretwork pieces H. Mark for nail placement by placing a pencil dot on the top beam and the fretwork piece.

4. Drill and nail end fretwork H to the top beam G, and to the outside of leg A, as pictured.

5. Repeat with the opposite side.

6. Arrange center fretwork I. Mark the pieces for nail placement as in step 3 above.

7. Begin with both center fretwork pieces and join them together at their junction point. Now fit the I assembly in place and join to the back legs at the pencil marks, remembering to drill pilot holes first.

8. Bevel the ends of the front split branch seat trim parts K as in step 2 above. Arrange the front seat trim in place and nail to the seat.

9. Arrange side seat trim in place (with mitered corners meeting), and nail in place.

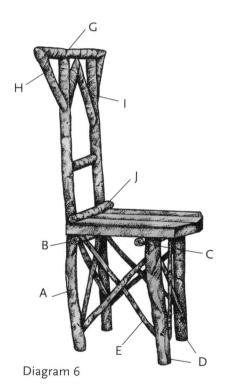

Diagram 6

Tree Chair

SKILL LEVEL: EXPERIENCED

HERE IS AN enchanting chair for the garden, the potting shed, or the front foyer. The seat is upholstered with a piece of vintage crazy quilt. If you plan to use the chair outside, leave the wood seat unadorned, or add personality with a piece of watertight fabric, such as striped awning canvas.

CUTTING CHART

NAME OF PART	QUANTITY	DIAMETER (INCHES)	LENGTH (INCHES)	DESCRIPTION
Legs A	3	1½–2	18–20	splayed hardwood
Coat-tree leg B	1	1½–2	80–90	splayed/multi-branched
Seat sides C	2	3	15	hardwood
Front seat stretcher D	1	2	15½	hardwood
Back seat stretcher E	1	2	14	hardwood
Seat supports F	2	½–¾	15	straight hardwood

TOOLS

- Single bit axe for felling trees
- Coping saw, skill saw, or belt sander
- Ruler or measuring tape
- Drill with a selection of bits
- Safety goggles

- Crosscut handsaw
- Clippers or garden shears
- Marking pencil
- Hammer
- Work gloves

MATERIALS

White birch, hickory, beech, or any hardwood branches ranging in length from 14" to 20" and from 1½" to 2" in diameter are suitable for the basic structure. One multi-branched twig, 70" to 90" long and 1½" to 2" in diameter, is needed for the coat-tree part of the chair. NOTE: The four legs, including the coat-tree leg, splay out at the bottom. Two hardwood branches, 3" in diameter and 15" long, are used for the seat sides in addition to two ½" to ¾" branches, 15" long for the seat supports. You will also need a 14" × 16" piece of lumber (¾" plywood) for the seat. Eight #40 spikes and four larger spikes, ⅜" diameter and 6" long, are needed to assemble the chair frame. You will also need a few finishing nails.

DIRECTIONS

Cutting the Branches

1. Cut three 1½" to 2" diameter hardwood branches for the legs A, each 18" to 20" long. NOTE: The back right leg is taller than the two front legs, and it splays outward at the top as well as the bottom.
2. Cut one ½" to 2" diameter multi-branched hardwood branch for the coat-tree leg B, 70" to 90" long.
3. Cut two 3" diameter branches for the seat sides C, each 15" long.
4. Cut one 2" diameter branch for the front seat stretcher D, 15½" long.
5. Cut one 2" diameter branch for the back seat stretcher E, 14" long.
6. Cut two ½" to ¾" diameter branches for the seat supports F, each 15" long.

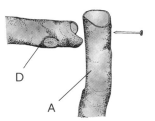

Diagram 1

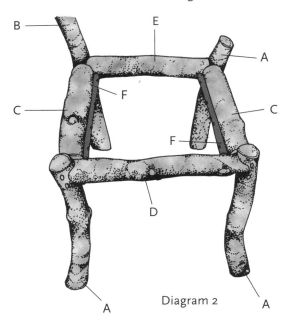

Diagram 2

Laying Out the Sub-Assembly

1. Arrange the front seat stretcher D between the two front legs A. Mark the sections to be carved on both ends of the front seat stretcher, and using the belt sander or coping saw, create the necessary shape required to fit part D against the two front legs A (diagram 1).
2. Butt the front seat stretcher D between both front legs A. Drill a pilot hole, and nail in place with 6" spikes (diagram 1).
3. Arrange the back seat stretcher E between the back leg A and the coat-tree leg B. Mark the ends of the back seat stretcher as in step 1 above.
4. Butt the back seat stretcher E between the back leg and the coat-tree leg B. Drill a pilot hole and nail in place as in step 2 above.

Joining the Sub-Assemblies

1. Butt one seat side C between one front leg A and the back leg A. Drill two holes through the front leg, approximately 1½" apart, and nail in place with two 6" spikes (diagram 2).
2. Drill two holes through the back leg and nail in place as in step 1 above.
3. Butt the remaining side seat C between the front leg A and the coat-tree leg B. Drill holes and nail in place as in steps 1 and 2 above.

Adding the Seat Supports

1. Position one seat support F against one seat side C. Drill pilot holes through the seat support, partway through the seat side C, and nail in place (diagram 3).
2. Repeat with the opposite side.

Making the Seat

Cut ¾" lumber to fit inside stretchers C, D, and E. NOTE: The seat rests on the seat supports F. A wood seat may be left to weather naturally, painted, or stained.

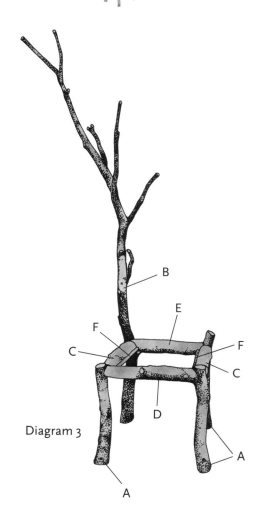

Diagram 3

Gothic
Arm Chair

I love it, I love it; and who shall dare
To chide me for loving that old arm-chair?

ELIZA COOK, 1818—1889

SKILL LEVEL: EXPERIENCED

TAKING A CUE from historical European gardens, this gothic-inspired arm chair is sure to become a favorite. The intimate connection between tree and furniture becomes obvious when you notice how few limbs are needed for this project. You will have to alter the design somewhat to accommodate your particular branches, but the plans are easy to adapt and you will want to make this sculptural chair for your retreat or garden.

CUTTING CHART

NAME OF PART	QUANTITY	DIAMETER (INCHES)	LENGTH (INCHES)	DESCRIPTION
Back legs/back A	2	1–2	47	hardwood
Front legs/arms B	2	1–2	47–51	natural forked & bent

NOTE: Part B is more than one piece; the arms are graceful branches growing out of the front legs. The chair's left front leg is 26" long, and its extended arm is minimum 22" long. The right front leg is 26" long and forked; its extended (attached) wrap-around arm/backrest is minimum 24" long.

NAME OF PART	QUANTITY	DIAMETER (INCHES)	LENGTH (INCHES)	DESCRIPTION
Seat trim C	3	½–1	10–16	willow (or any hardwood)
Seat	1	1½-thick	13 × 16	fir

NOTE: The seat measures 16" at the front edge and 13" at the back. It is made from two two-by-eights.

TOOLS

• Single bit axe for felling trees	• Crosscut hand saw
• Clippers or garden shears	• Ruler or measuring tape
• Marking pencil	• Drill with a selection of bits
• Hammer	• Safety goggles
• Work gloves	

MATERIALS

Use such woods as beech, cedar, cherry, or maple. Lengths will range from 25" to 47" and 1" to 2" in diameter for the chair, and ¾" diameter branches, 10" to 15" long for the trim. You will want to have a good selection of multi-branched and forked pieces, for it is in this combination of parts that a unique chair will be built. Trees at the edge of dense woods are often bent into distorted shapes in their fight for survival, and the natural twists and turns of their branches are what you want to add grace and style to your design. One or two pieces of 1½" pine totaling 13" × 16" will be required for the seat. Have a selection of galvanized 1½" nails, and 1½" finishing nails, and you are ready to begin.

DIRECTIONS

Cutting the Basic Branches

1. Carefully select two similarly shaped 1" to 2" diameter branches for the back legs/back A, each approximately 47" long, allowing for final leg trimming, and the arched construction.

2. Carefully select two natural forked and curved branches for the front legs/arms B, each approximately 47" to 51" long, allowing for trimming and fitting.

Making the Seat

Join two 16" two-by-eights parallel with two two-by-fours across the underside. NOTE: The seat tapers from 16" across the front to 13" across the back. Lay the two-by-eights side-by-side on the work table. Locate the center of the boards, measure 6½" to either side of center across the back, and draw lines from these points to the front corners (diagram 1). Nail a two-by-four along both these lines (diagram 2). Finally, cut round notches in all four corners of the seat to hold the legs (diagram 3).

Diagram 1

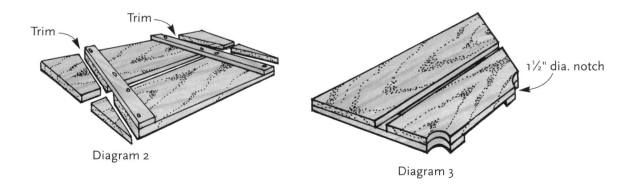

Diagram 2

Diagram 3

1½" dia. notch

Building the Back

1. Using a pencil, mark the inside of both back legs A, 17" from the bottom.
2. Position the seat (13" end) between the two back legs A at the pencil marks.
3. Drill pilot holes and nail the back legs to the seat.
4. Slightly bend legs/back parts A at the top; slice at an angle and fit together, forming the gothic arch. Drill pilot holes and nail in place (diagram 4).

Diagram 4

Adding the Front Legs/Arms

1. Using a pencil, mark the inside of both front legs/arms B, 17" from the bottom. NOTE: The arms should branch from the legs at approximately 7" above the seat.
2. Position the seat (16" end) at the 17" front leg/arm point. Drill pilot holes and nail the front legs in place. Adjust the extending arms in place, and nail them with pilot holes at a point where they naturally cross the legs/back parts A (diagram 5).

Adding the Seat Trim

1. Cut two ½" diameter twigs (seat trim C), long enough to fit between the front and back legs along the sides of the seat. Using three finishing nails each, drill pilot holes and nail them in place (diagram 5).
2. Cut one 1" diameter twig, 16" long for the front seat trim C. Nail in place as above.

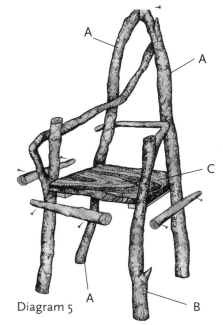

Diagram 5

Revamped Rocking Chair

To make good use of idle time in the winter, when there is but little to do in the garden, cut the wood for rustic chairs and tables.

PETERSON'S MAGAZINE
NOVEMBER, 1856

A ROCKING CHAIR is perfect in the flower garden—I just wish I had thought of it sooner! Gleaned from a yard sale, this timeworn treasure takes on new life with a simple twig-stringing technique. Once you discover how easy it is to repair chairs with this method, you will be searching for forgotten pieces to turn into tomorrow's heirlooms. Build the jig and adjust the spacing for your particular chair; for the seat only, for the back only, or for seat and back as in the rocker pictured.

NAME OF PART	QUANTITY	DIAMETER (INCHES)	LENGTH (INCHES)	DESCRIPTION
Twigs (back)	32	½–¾	15	straight
Twigs (seat)	15	½–¾	16–21	straight
Arms	2	1	25	bent

CUTTING CHART

TOOLS

• Axe or saw for cutting trees	• Crosscut hand saw
• Ruler	• Marking pencil
• Drill and a selection of bits	• Wire clippers

MATERIALS

NOTE: The following materials are for the specific chair illustrated. This antique chair originally had a caned back and seat, and therefore has pre-drilled holes along the rim surrounding the back and the seat. The threaded twig wires are inserted through these holes.

Use such wood as willow, beech, birch, or hickory. You will need 32 straight twigs, 15" long and ½" to ¾" in diameter for the back. You will need 15 straight twigs, 16" to 21" long and ½" to ¾" in diameter for the seat. You will also need four straight wires, approximately 30" long and ¹⁄₁₆" in diameter; two pieces of board, approximately 20" long to make the jigs; and one large nail to use with the jigs. Two bent 1" diameter branches are used for the arms.

DIRECTIONS

Cutting the Branches

1. Cut thirty-two 1" diameter branches, 15" long for the back.
2. Cut fifteen 1" diameter branches, 16" to 21" long for the seat. NOTE: The length of the seat branches varies to accommodate the shape of the seat, while the back opening is uniform.

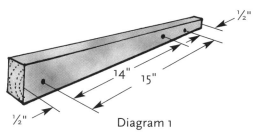

½"

14" 15"

½"

Diagram 1

Diagram 2

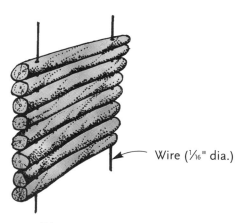

Wire (⅟₁₆" dia.)

Diagram 3

Making the Jig

One 16" long one-by-three board can be used for both sets of branches. For the back, drill two ⅛" diameter holes 14" apart and for the seat, drill a second hole 17" away from the first one (diagram 1).

Drilling the Branches

1. In 32 of the branches, drill holes 14" apart. Center them using the jig as your guide (diagram 2). (NOTE: To drill the second hole in each twig, place a nail in the first drilled hole through the jig into the branch. This holds the jig in place and ensures accuracy.) Make sure the diameter of the hole is large enough to allow you to thread the ⅟₁₆" wire through the hole.

2. In 15 of the branches, drill holes 15" apart. Center them using the jig as your guide, as you did in step 1.

Stringing the Twigs

String the drilled branches onto two straight pieces of wire. Place the first branch in the middle of both wires. Continue stringing from both directions equally, until the wire is covered with enough branches to fully cover the back or seat (diagram 3). There should be approximately 5" to 10" of wire at each end of the threaded twigs. These wire ends will be inserted in the chair's cane holes.

Arranging the Back

1. Cut two straight wires to string the 32 back branches, leaving an extra 10" to allow for attaching the twigs to the chair.
2. String the 32 (back) drilled branches onto two straight pieces of wire.
3. Bend the wire at each end of the threaded twigs, and insert the wires through the back rim chair holes at the top and at the bottom. To secure the end of each wire, drill a pilot hole into the back of the chair and turn a round-head screw partway in (near the wire end) and wrap the wire tightly around the nail (diagram 4). Using wire clippers, cut the ends of the wires.

Diagram 4

Arranging the Seat

1. Cut two straight wires to string the 15 seat branches, leaving ten extra inches to allow for attaching the twigs to the chair.
2. String the 15 (seat) drilled branches onto two straight pieces of wire.
3. Bend the bare wire at each end of the threaded twigs, and insert the wires through the seat rim holes at the front, and at the back of the seat opening. Secure the wire ends in the same manner as the back wire ends (diagram 4).

Adding the Arms

The one-piece bent branches that make up the arms are nailed or screwed to the chair back at a convenient location: approximately 9" up from the seat; and to the seat side-front at approximately 10" up from the leg bottom.

Easy-Seat Red Rocker

O, my luve's like a red, red rose
That's newly sprung in June.

ROBERT BURNS

SKILL LEVEL: BEGINNER

HERE IS ANOTHER yard sale rocker, this time transformed with a simple seat-making technique that you can use on many types of chairs and seating. Between the simple technique discussed here and the technique from the Revamped Rocking Chair, you will be able to make yourself a whole new set of chairs for garden dining.

CUTTING CHART

NAME OF PART	QUANTITY	DIAMETER (INCHES)	LENGTH (INCHES)	DESCRIPTION
Front to back seat parts	5	⅜	15	straight/hardwood
Side to side seat parts	6	⅜	14"–17"	straight/hardwood

TOOLS

• Crosscut hand saw	• Clippers or garden shears
• Ruler	• Marking pencil
• Drill and a selection of bits	• Hammer
• Safety goggles	• Work gloves

MATERIALS

NOTE: These directions are for a seat with a double row of rungs. If your chair seat has a single frame, attach the seat branches to the frame itself (diagram 1). The following materials are for the chair illustrated which is 14" deep × 17" at the front × 14" at the back. Adjust the materials for your particular chair. Use willow, dogwood, beech, birch, or hickory twigs, ⅜" in diameter and approximately 17" long. Use 1" finishing nails or panel nails to complete the seat.

DIRECTIONS

Cutting the Branches

1. Cut five ⅜" diameter branches, 15" long for the "front-to-back" seat parts A.
2. Cut six ⅜" diameter branches, from 14" to 17" long for the "side-to-side" seat parts B.

Arranging the Seat

1. Install the five "front-to-back" seat parts A, equally spaced, between the two existing front and back rungs as pictured in diagram 2.
2. NOTE: The front two seat parts measure 17", the center two measure 16", and the back two measure 14". Lay the six "side-to-side" seat parts B over

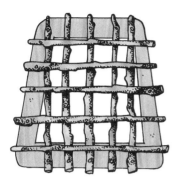

Diagram 1

Diagram 2

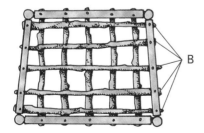

Diagram 3

the first set of six branches, and between the side rungs as shown in diagram 3.

3. Drill pilot holes from the top along the top front chair rung, where it meets the five seat parts A. Nail in place.

4. Repeat step 3 above with the back chair rung.

5. Drill pilot holes from the top along the top side chair rungs where they meet the six seat parts B, and nail in place. NOTE: If your branches are straight, and strong and tight between the seat's parallel rungs, it is not necessary to nail the branches at every junction.

Canopy Bench with Bluestone Seat

*Seats to be comfortable, will need to have cushions
made of some stout material, such as heavy canvas, and
stuffed with twigs of evergreen, white birch bark or shavings.*

WILLIAM S. WICKS,
"LOG CABINS AND COTTAGES"

SKILL LEVEL: EXPERIENCED

HERE IS A versatile piece that can be customized to meet your needs. This
sturdy cedar bench, shown here with a canopy top, is perfect for sunny summer days in open areas along the shore or garden path. It can, however, be
built without the top and serve as a solid seat under an arbor or any spot
where shade is not required. Although this bench has a naturally formed
bluestone seat, the bench would also welcome a wood plank or a padded
foam rubber, canvas-covered seat or wooden slats. In this case, the canopy
and seat are made of an outdoor canvas material reminiscent of grandma's
vintage lawn furniture, in a traditional dark green, red, and white stripe.

CUTTING CHART

NAME OF PART	QUANTITY	DIAMETER (INCHES)	LENGTH (INCHES)	DESCRIPTION
Front legs A	2	2–3	29	hardwood
Back legs B	2	2–3	72	hardwood, forked
Front/back beams C	2	2½	52	hardwood
Top side beams D	2	2	12	hardwood
Bottom side beams E	2	2	12	hardwood
Seat backs F	2	2	60–62	hardwood
Arms G	2	2–3	29	hardwood, split
Seat supports H	3	2–3	56	hardwood, split
Bottom braces I	2–3	1–1½	60–70	hardwood, supple
Front/back canopy frame J	2	1–2	21	hardwood
Side canopy frame K	2	1–2	36	hardwood

*Try to find poles with natural forks to support the canopy frame. If you are unable to locate forked branches of this size, use diagonal braces to guarantee a strong structure.

TOOLS

- Single bit axe for felling trees or an electric chain saw
- ⅜" variable-speed drill and a selection of bits

• Crosscut hand saw	• Garden shears or clippers
• Hammer	• Measuring tape
• Marking pencil	• Level
• Safety goggles	• Work gloves

MATERIALS

Cedar, beech, birch, or any hardwood poles ranging in lengths from 12" to 70" and from 1" to 3" in diameter are suitable for this bench. You will also need a seat. This large solid piece of bluestone, 11" × 13" and 1½" thick, was a rare find. I was also grateful that my husband was available to transport it and lay it in place. For an easier solution, use an 11" × 13" piece of wood, 1" to 2" thick. NOTE: The bluestone seat is not attached to the bench. It simply rests on three split 2" to 3" diameter logs, 52" long. You will also need galvanized flathead nails in assorted sizes (#6p, #8p, #10p, #12p, and #16p) to complete the project.

DIRECTIONS

Cutting the Branches

1. Cut two 2" to 3" diameter branches for the front legs A, each 29" long.
2. Cut two 2" to 3" diameter branches for the back legs B, each 72" long.
3. Cut two 2½" diameter branches for the front/back beams C, each 52" long.
4. Cut two 2" diameter branches for the top side beams D, each 12" long.
5. Cut two 2" diameter branches for the seat backs F, each 60" to 62" long.
6. Cut and split one 2" to 3" diameter branch for the arms G, 29" long.
7. Cut and split three 2" to 3" diameter branches for the seat supports H, each 51" long.
8. Cut two or three 2" to 3" diameter supple branches for the bottom braces I, each 60" to 70" long.
9. Cut two 1" to 2" diameter branches for the front canopy frame J, each 21" long.
10. Cut two 1" to 2" diameter branches for the side canopy frame K, each 36" long.

Laying Out the Sub-Assembly

1. Butt one beam C between both front legs A, 18" up from the bottom of the legs. Using pilot holes, nail in place from the outside of each leg (diagram 1).
2. Butt the remaining beam C between both back legs B, 18" up from the bottom of the legs. Nail in place as in step 1 above.
3. Lay the back leg/beam construction down (front down/back up) on a work surface. Position one seat back F across both back legs approximately 10" up from beam C.

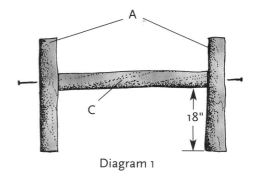

Diagram 1

4. Drill and nail seat back E in place through the back into the back legs B.
5. Lay the remaining seat back E across both back legs at a location approximately 6" from the installed seat back. Drill and nail in place as in step 4 above (diagram 2).

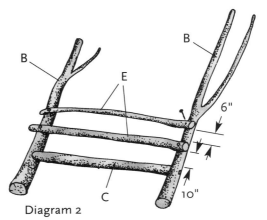

Diagram 2

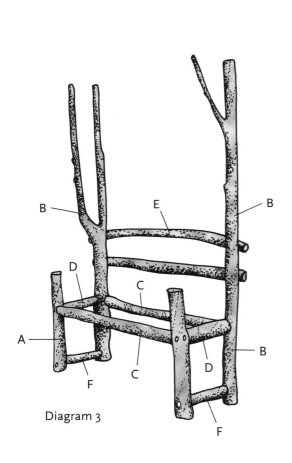

Diagram 3

Joining the Sub-Assemblies

1. Butt one top side beam D between the inside of the front and back legs approximately 18" from the bottom of the leg. Using pilot holes, nail in place through the front of the front leg and the back of the back leg.
2. Repeat with the opposite side.
3. Butt one bottom side beam F between the inside of the front and back legs approximately 4" from the bottom of the leg. Drill a pilot hole, and nail in place as shown in step 1 above.
4. Repeat with the opposite side (diagram 3).

5. Nail one arm G (split side down) to the top of the front leg and to the seat back E.
6. Repeat with the other arm (diagram 4).

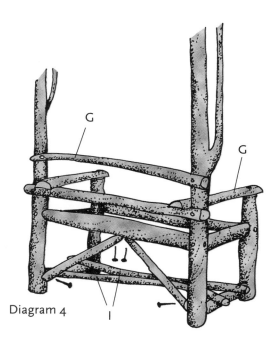

Diagram 4

Adding the Seat Supports

1. NOTE: The three seat supports H are attached under both side beams D, with the split side facing up. Place the construction on its back and position one seat support, split side up, across both side beams approximately 4" from the back legs. Drill a pilot hole and nail in place.
2. Repeat step 1 with the remaining two seat supports H, spacing them approximately 2" to 3" apart.

Adding the Bottom Beams

NOTE: Use supple branches for the bottom braces to help support and strengthen the structure.

1. Place one bottom brace I against the inside of the two front legs, and on top of both bottom beams. Drill and nail in place.
2. Place the remaining bottom brace I against the inside of the two back legs B and on the top of the bottom beams. Drill and nail in place as above.

Adding the Canopy Frame

1. Butt one side canopy frame K between both front/back canopy frames J. Drill and nail in place.
2. Repeat step 1 above with the remaining side canopy frame K (diagram 5).

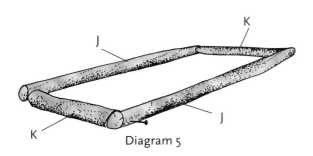

Diagram 5

3. The canopy framework is nailed to the 72" tall back legs, from the top of the legs and the top of the extended natural forks.

The Canopy

There are several ways to attach a cloth canopy. The most simple solution requires a piece of outdoor canvas approximately 56" × 38", tacked in place along the edge of the canopy frame. Add an awning skirt, 6" to 8" deep, along the circumference of the framework. Alternatively, you can use a canvas canopy framed with grommets and tie it to the canopy frame with rope. In this case the canvas is hemmed on all sides with a 1 ½" hem and grommets are placed in the four corners and equally spaced around the perimeter as shown in diagram 6.

When making a canvas canopy, one or two slightly arched slender willow

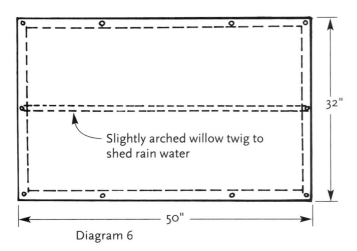

Slightly arched willow twig to shed rain water

32"

50"

Diagram 6

branches applied between the canopy frame end pieces K are needed to help it shed rain water. Use pilot holes and headless nails to fasten the arched willow branches in place.

For a natural canopy, add several straight branches to the canopy frame and weave supple vines and branches over and under the arrangement.

The Seat

Lay the stone or wooden seat down on the installed seat supports H. Check to make certain that the seat is stable. To guarantee a level seat, it may be necessary to attach one or two branches between the seat and the seat supports.

To build the padded foam rubber canvas-covered seat, start with a pine board approximately 50" long and 9" wide; ¾" thickess is adequate. A piece of foam rubber material of the same size, 9" × 50" and 2" to 3" thick, will work well. Place the foam rubber on top of the board and the large canvas on top of the foam. The canvas should be 20" to 60" so it can be wrapped around the foam and board. Tack the canvas to the underside of the board.

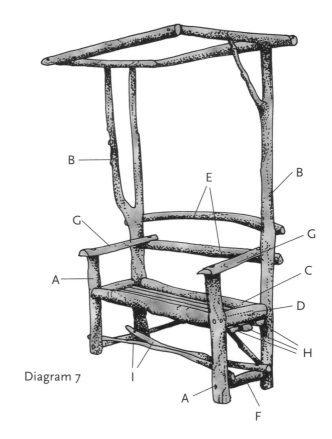

Diagram 7

Folding Bench

I know a little garden close,
Set thick with lily and red rose,
Where I could wander
If I might
From dewy morn
To dewy night.

WILLIAM MORRIS

PERFECT FOR GARDENERS with limited space, this practical folding bench is easily stored when not in use. Amid a flower garden, topped with a wooden plank it is ideal for a summer picnic. Whether you use it to support bushel baskets when you are gathering your garden bounty, or to hold potted geraniums on the porch, I know you will want to try your hand at a rustic twig folding bench.

202

CUTTING CHART

NAME OF PART	QUANTITY	DIAMETER (INCHES)	LENGTH (INCHES)	DESCRIPTION
Top beams A	3	1¼–1¾	44	straight, hardwood
Legs B	4	1¼–1¾	21	straight, hardwood
Top rail C	2	1–1½	20	straight, hardwood
Bottom rail D	2	1–1½	17	straight, hardwood
Wood dowels	3	¾–1	16	

TOOLS

• Single bit axe for felling trees	• Crosscut hand saw
• Clippers	• Ruler or measuring tape
• Marking pencil	• Hammer
• Drill with a selection of bits	• Safety goggles
• Work gloves	

MATERIALS

Use straight hardwood branches such as birch, hickory, or willow. Lengths will range from 17" to 44" and diameters from 1¼" to 1¾". Three hardwood dowels, 16" long and ¾" to 1" in diameter, are required for the construction, along with galvanized flathead nails in assorted sizes.

DIRECTIONS

Cutting the Branches

1. Cut three 1¼" to 1¾" diameter straight branches for the top beams A, each 44" long.
2. Cut four 1¼" to 1¾" diameter straight branches for the legs B, each 21" long.
3. Cut two 1" to 1½" diameter straight branches for the top rails C, each 20" long.
4. Cut two 1" to 1½" diameter straight branches for the bottom rails C1, each 17" long.
5. Cut three ¾" to 1" diameter wood dowels 16" long.

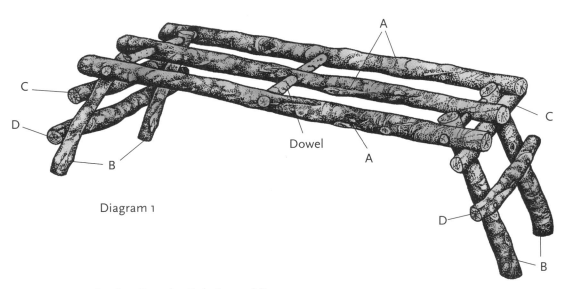

Diagram 1

Laying Out the Sub-Assemblies

NOTE: The top beams A are the "stops" that permit the bench to stand up-right, and must extend beyond the top rails C when joined. For this project you will want to read all directions before beginning.

1. Place the three top beams A on the workbench. Using the pencil, mark a location at the center (22") on each beam.

2. Using the drill and correct bit, drill a hole with the same diameter as the dowel through each beam at the center mark.

3. Arrange the three top beams A, parallel on the workbench approximately 8" apart. Insert the dowel through all three top beams. Drill pilot holes and nail the dowel in place through the A beams, from the bottom (diagram 1). Set the top sub-assembly aside.

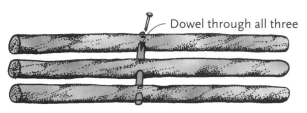

Dowel through all three

Diagram 1

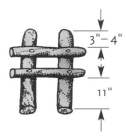

3"– 4"

11"

Diagram 2

4. Place two legs B, parallel on the workbench approximately 15" apart. Overlap top rail C across both legs, 3" to 4" down from the top of the legs. Drill pilot holes and nail in place.

5. Overlap bottom rail D across both legs, 11" from the bottom of both legs. Drill pilot holes and nail in place (diagram 2).

6. Repeat steps 4 and 5 with the remaining legs B, and rails C and D.

Joining the Sub-Assemblies

1. Place one leg assembly on the workbench along with the top assembly. Position the two legs B inside the two exterior top beams A, and check to make sure that the three top beams rest on top of the top rail C (diagram 3). NOTE: The top rails are the "stops" that permit the bench to stand upright.

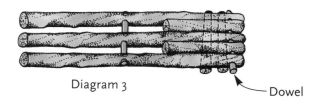

Diagram 3 — Dowel

2. Using a pencil mark a spot along legs B, 1½" to 2" from the top. Drill a hole the same diameter as the dowel at these spots.

3. Repeat steps 1 and 2 above with the remaining leg assemblies.

4. At a location 3" from the ends of each of the three top beams A, drill holes ⅛" larger than the dowel's diameter. Remember, drilling the holes ⅛" larger than the diameter of the dowel makes folding the bench easy.

5. Position the legs B, inside the exterior top beams and insert the dowel through the three top rails and legs to form a pivot. Try folding the legs at this point to make sure they move easily. Correct the drilled hole diameter if necessary. When you are satisfied with the placement, turn the construction over and nail the dowels in place through the top beams using pilot hole construction. Repeat with the opposite side.

Forked Garden Seat

As violets recluse and sweet,
Cheerful as daisies unaccounted rare;
Still sunward gazing from a lowly seat;
Still sweetening wintry air.

CHRISTINA ROSSETTI

SKILL LEVEL: BEGINNER

CRAFT THIS three-legged forked-back chair from an appropriate branch and create a special resting spot in the garden. Easy to carry and well balanced, this chair fits almost anywhere and adds interest wherever it is placed. A descendant of the English walking chair, garden enthusiasts will welcome its simple design.

CUTTING CHART

NAME OF PART	QUANTITY	DIAMETER (INCHES)	LENGTH (INCHES)	DESCRIPTION
Back leg A	1	1½	40	forked hardwood
Front legs B	2	1	18	hardwood
Seat	1	12		2" thick seasoned wood, such as cherry, maple, pine, or oak

TOOLS

- Single bit axe for felling trees
- Crosscut hand saw
- Ruler or measuring tape
- Marking pencil
- ⅜" variable-speed drill with a selection of bits
- Sandpaper (or electric sander)
- Wood glue (optional)
- Safety goggles and work gloves

Diagram 1

MATERIALS

You will need three hardwood branches, including one forked branch, such as birch or beech, ranging from 18" to 40", and with a 1½" diameter for leg A and a 1" diameter for legs B. You will also need a log slice, 2" thick and approximately 12" in diameter. NOTE: Log slices can be obtained from a logger, tree-trimming service, or firewood supplier. Thick wood planks from the lumber yard also work. You will also need wood glue for the front legs and two 1¾" finishing nails for the back leg.

DIRECTIONS

1. Cut one forked 1½" diameter branch for the back leg A, 40" long.
2. Cut two 1" diameter branches for the front legs B, each 18" long.
3. Prepare the 12" diameter wood slab by sanding the surfaces smooth.

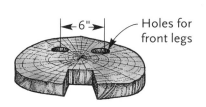

Diagram 2 Underside of seat

4. Cut a 1½" square notch from the back of the wood slab seat to give the back leg A a snug fit.

Attaching the Front Legs to the Seat

1. Lay the slab-seat face down on a work table. Using a pencil, mark the slab at the two spots where the front legs will be inserted, 2½" in from the sides and 6" apart at approximately 3" from the front of the seat.
2. Drill holes approximately 1¼" deep at the pencil marks. NOTE: Holes should be slightly smaller than the twig to allow for a snug fit.
3. Hammer the legs into the drilled holes and adjust their length as necessary to guarantee a level chair. If you want to, add a squirt of wood glue in the holes and dab some on the ends of the legs. Dip the ends of the legs in sawdust if they are loose.

Attaching the Back Leg

Position the back leg in the previously cut U-shaped seat back opening. The legs stand 16" to 17" tall from floor to seat; because the front legs splay slightly outward, they are approximately 17" and the back leg is approximately 16" tall.

Using pilot holes and two 1¾" galvanized common nails, attach the back leg A to the seat.

Stand the chair upright and trim the bottom of the back leg if necessary.

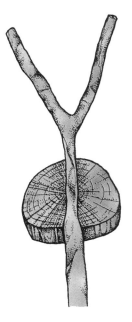

Diagram 3 Back leg A

CHAPTER 7

A Baker's Dozen Quick & Easy Projects

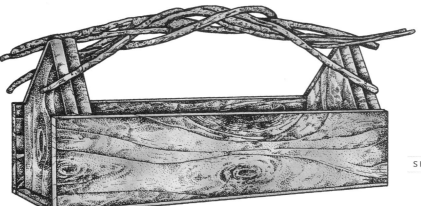

SKILL LEVEL: BEGINNER

Twig=Handled Garden Tool Carrier

Some morning in May I sit in the sunshine and soft air,
transplanting my young Pansies and Gillyflowers
into the garden beds…

CELIA THAXTER,
AN ISLAND GARDEN

BUILT LIKE a carpenter's tool box, this twig-handled version is perfect for transporting your most frequently used items, such as a hand shovel, a weeder, your clippers, or your gloves. It is just as useful for carrying weeds to the compost pile, or greens to the kitchen, and it makes a nice planter.

CUTTING CHART

NAME OF PART	QUANTITY	DIAMETER (INCHES)	LENGTH (INCHES)	DESCRIPTION
Sides A ½" thick	2	5	25	Seasoned lumber
Bottom B ½" thick	1	5	25	Seasoned lumber
Ends C ¾" thick	2	5	9	Seasoned lumber
Handle D	1	¾-dia.	22	Pliable twig
Handle wraps E	4–6	¼–½	30	Pliable twigs
Trim F	4	1-dia.	5½	Hardwood twig/split

TOOLS

- Crosscut hand saw
- Ruler
- Drill with a selection of bits
- Safety goggles
- Garden shears or clippers
- Pencil
- Hammer
- Work gloves

MATERIALS

You will need five pieces of ½" to ¾" thick lumber in lengths from 9" to 25" and 5" wide. Almost any kind of wood may be used, from weathered barn siding to seasoned oak, or a good quality pine from the lumber yard. The carrier pictured is made of old rough-sawed hemlock weathered to a nice silver grey color. You will also need an assortment of 30" long flexible ("green") twigs, with diameters from ¼" to ¾", along with galvanized flathead nails and 1" finishing nails.

DIRECTIONS

Cutting the End Pieces

1. Measure 5" from the bottom of an end piece C, and using a pencil, mark both sides at this point. Repeat with the second end piece.
2. With the ruler and pencil, divide an end piece in half, and draw a line from top to bottom. Repeat with the second end piece.
3. Cut one end piece, at a slant from the top mid-point line to the 5" pencil mark. Repeat with the other side, forming the triangular top shape. Repeat with the remaining end piece.

Building the Carrier

1. Arrange one end piece C along the bottom B, allowing approximately ¾" of the bottom to extend. Join the end to the bottom, with a pilot hole and nail, from the underside with 1½" galvanized nails (or any nails of choice guaranteeing a tight joint). Repeat with the other end piece on the opposite end of the bottom.

2. Join one side A to both end pieces with three 1½" galvanized nails, drilling pilot holes through the sides into the end piece. Repeat with the remaining side. NOTE: The sides, like the bottom, extend beyond the end pieces approximately ¾".

Adding the Handle and the Trim

1. Measure the inside distance between both ends C. Cut a ¾" pliable branch slightly longer (approximately 2" longer) than the inside distance. This permits the handle's shape to be formed.

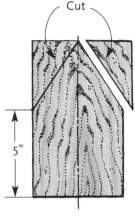

Cut

5"

Diagram 1

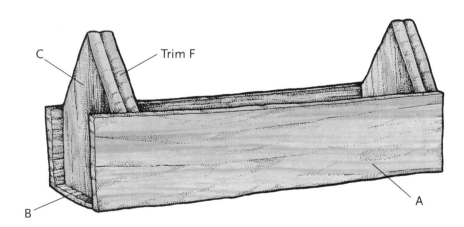

C

Trim F

B

A

Diagram 2

2. Make a mark approximately 1" down from the top of both ends C, on the inside and the outside. Join the handle at the mark, using a pilot hole and nail, nailing from the outside. Carefully bend the handle to be joined at the other end; bevel the end of the pliable twig to fit flush with the end if necessary, and join as above.

3. Cut four 1" diameter twigs approximately 5½" long for the trim F. Split them in half, and nail them to the angled tops of the end pieces, drilling a pilot hole beforehand and using galvanized finishing nails.

4. Carefully bend ¼" to ¾" flexible twigs over and under the attached handle, permitting the twig ends to extend beyond the carrier. Tack some of these in place using thin finishing nails; others will be able to stay put once they dry.

Diagram 3

D

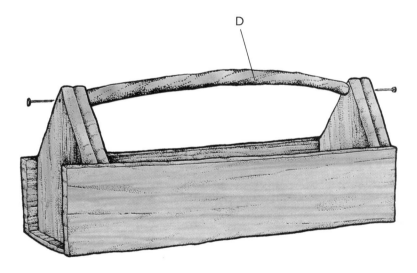

Diagram 4

Star Pocket Planter

Rofemarie is fpice in the German kitchens, and other cold countries.

JOHN GERARD,
THE HERBALL, 1597

THIS LITTLE STAR pocket planter helps to preserve a winter memory of a woodland walk where sheets of fallen birch bark were brought home and applied to scrap wood. It is a charming front door decoration holding dried herbs and grasses, or add hemlock boughs and pinecones for a festive winter wallhanging.

T O O L S

• Clippers or garden shears	• Keyhole saw and coping saw
• Scissors	• Work gloves
• Wooden mallet (required for bark peeling)	• Ruler or measuring tape
• Marking pencil	• Hammer
• 1" wide straight chisel (required for bark peeling)	

MATERIALS

You will need an assortment of peeled bark sheets, with two sheets at least 11" wide (see pattern); and two pieces of ⅛" plywood, each 11" × 11". One straight branch, at least 7" long and ¼" diameter, is required, along with epoxy glue (or a glue gun) and ½" finishing nails.

DIRECTIONS

Applying the Bark

1. Enlarge the pattern to the desired size. Trace both outlines, front and back, of the star pattern on the scrap lumber, and using the coping saw, cut out one full star shape and one partial front pocket star.
2. Trace the star outlines on the bark, and cut the bark with scissors.
3. Trace the triangle opening on the plywood and the bark, and using the keyhole saw cut out both openings (this is for hanging the planter).
4. Lay the plywood back star face up on a work surface. Attach the bark to the plywood with the glue or glue gun. Affix bark to the front star with glue from a bottle or glue gun. If using glue you'll need clothespins to hold the bark in place for several hours.

Forming the Pocket

1. Cut a ¼" diameter twig into seven 1" lengths.
2. Place the 1" spacer twigs along the outside edge of the back star (see diagram) and using the finishing nails, nail in place from the back.

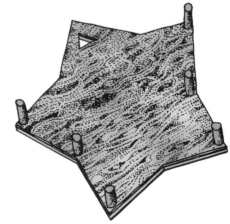

Diagram 1

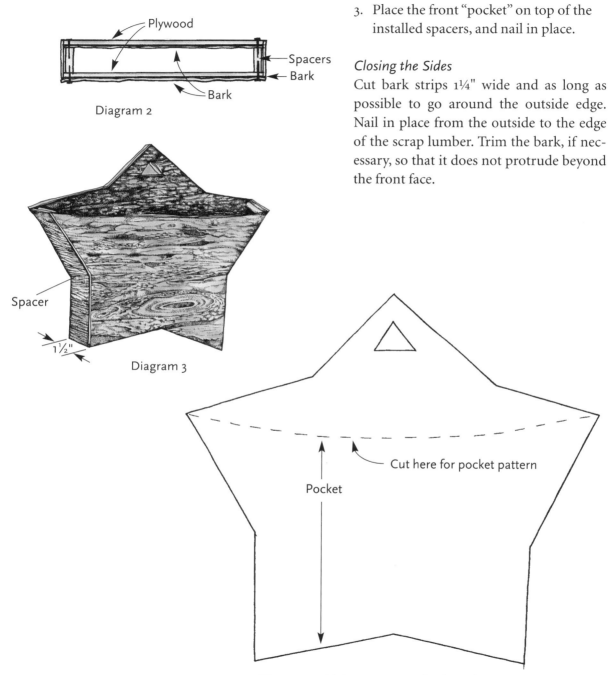

Diagram 2

Plywood

Spacers

Bark

Bark

Diagram 3

Spacer

1½"

3. Place the front "pocket" on top of the installed spacers, and nail in place.

Closing the Sides

Cut bark strips 1¼" wide and as long as possible to go around the outside edge. Nail in place from the outside to the edge of the scrap lumber. Trim the bark, if necessary, so that it does not protrude beyond the front face.

Cut here for pocket pattern

Pocket

Diagram 2   Make 2 copies and enlarge by 200%.

Garden Markers

So we had a bit of garden ground made ready,
while the farmers about us sat by their fires
in the belief that it was yet winter…

DOROTHEA ALICE SHEPHERD, 1875

LABEL YOUR PLANTS the natural way with these whimsical markers that look as if they grew from the garden. The letters are formed with flexible twigs, and the stakes are whittled sticks. This is a good project for people with limited space and a welcomed gift for gardening friends.

217

TOOLS	
• Axe or saw for cutting trees	• Coping saw and/or keyhole saw
• Garden shears or clippers	• Sharp knife (optional)
• Scissors (for cutting bark)	• Ruler or measuring tape
• Marking pencil	• Drill with a selection of bits
• Tack hammer	• Staple gun (optional)
• Safety goggles	• Work gloves

MATERIALS

A walk in the woods can lead you to loose scraps of bark and appealing twigs and sticks that can be used for these garden markers. You will need a piece of scrap lumber, or a roofing shingle, and a 23" long stick for each marker. You will also need a piece of peeled birch bark at least 3" wide and 6" long. Use pliable twigs such as willow or alder for the lettering. Lengths range from 3" to 24", and twig diameters should be ⅛" to ½" for the letters, and ¼" to ¾" for the trim, and ½" to 1½" for the stakes. You should also have a variety of tacks and finishing nails for attaching the bark veneer, twig trim, and twig letters to the scrap lumber.

DIRECTIONS

NOTE: The directions that follow are suggestions on materials, methods, and measurements; rely on your own design sense to create individualistic garden markers. The number of letters helps to determine the size of the marker, and the plants usually dictate the height. A good average is 3" × 6" for the markers, and 10" to 2 ft. high for the stakes. The kale marker pictured is 3" × 6" and 1 ft. high, while basil is 3½" × 4½" and 14" high.

1. Form the letters with supple twigs, and attach them to the wood boards with thin finishing nails. For an attractive variation, birch bark can be affixed to a wood foundation with carpet tacks before adding twig lettering.
2. Trim the board edges with twigs and fasten with finishing nails.
3. Fix the stakes to the back of the boards with galvanized flathead nails (#2p, #4p, or #6p).
4. Using a sharp knife, whittle one end of the stake into a point to permit easy installation.

Look at the illustrations for inspiration, but be willing to change your plans as the work progresses; it's all part of the creative experience.

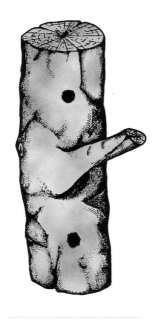

Handy Hooks

SKILL LEVEL: BEGINNER

Here in this sequestered close,
Bloom the hyacinth and the rose;
Here beside the modest stock
Flaunts the flaring hollyhock;
Here without pang, one sees
Ranks, conditions, and degrees.

AUSTIN DOBSON

A PERFECT PLACE to hang your garden hat, these handy natural branch hooks are simple to make. Install some in the potting shed to keep your tools off the floor and out of harm's way. Place some near the back door for aprons, smocks, and gardening clothes. Once you discover how these hooks help you tidy up your work area, you will be using them for lawn bags, watering cans, brooms, baskets, gloves, and the garden hose.

• Crosscut hand saw	• Ruler or measuring tape
• Marking pencil	• Electric drill and a variety of bits
• ¼" to ⅜" woodboring bit (optional, needed to countersink drill the holes)	• Screwdriver for installation
• Safety goggles	• Work gloves

MATERIALS

Choose a hardwood such as white birch, beech, maple, or cherry. All hooks require forked branches to form the natural peg. Individual handy hooks may vary in size from 8" to 1 ft., with 1" to 2" diameters. The hooks are installed with two screws.

DIRECTIONS

1. Measure and mark the length of the branch in half. Using a hand saw, cut the branch in half along the mark.

2. Measure and mark two points 1" to 2" from the ends of the branch for the installation holes. To make plugged screwholes, drill two ⅜" deep holes slightly larger than the head of the screw you plan to use. Drill a pilot hole for the screw through the center of the larger hole (diagram 1). After the screws are installed the holes may be plugged with pegs cut from twigs, thereby covering the screw heads.

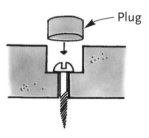

Diagram 1

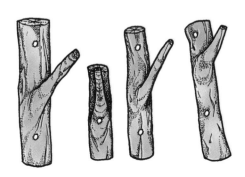

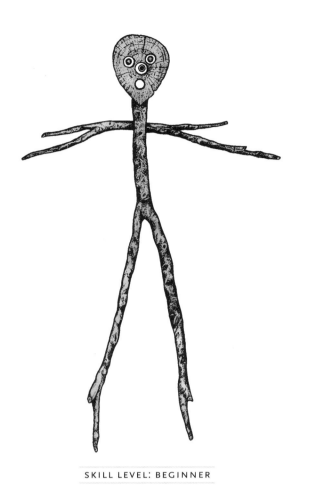

Scarecrow

*In the further field
A scarecrow kept me company,
Walking as I walked.*

SANIN, 17TH CENTURY HAIKU POET

ORIGINALLY USED to frighten crows or other birds away from crops, a scarecrow adds a bit of fanciful whimsy to any outdoor area. Scarecrows are easy to make out of twigs and branches with assorted found objects for facial features. This familiar figure is the perfect project for budding rustic designers looking for a garden centerpiece!

TOOLS

• Axe	• Crosscut hand saw
• Clippers or garden shears	• Ruler or measuring tape
• Marking pencil	• Drill with a selection of bits
• Hammer	• Safety goggles
• Work gloves	

MATERIALS

You will need a 3" thick wood slab, 13" in diameter for the head; two forked branches, 3 ft. long for the arms; and one 90" long forked branch for the body (including the legs). Adjust the measurements to suit your location. Use three branches for the body/leg part if you cannot locate one forked branch. Consider using one branch for the arms and adding multi-forked twigs for hands. Here a pair of bottle caps are used for the eyes and a brass hose nozzle for the nose. You will need a handful of galvanized nails to join the head and the arms to the body.

Diagram 1

DIRECTIONS

1. Place the wood slab (face) on the workbench. Mark the location for the eyes, 6" down and centered 5" apart. Drill holes and nail eyes in place. Bottle caps, jar lids, or political buttons make good eyes. Center nose on face and attach. The garden nozzle is attached with a nail. If you don't have an extra garden nozzle lying around, a twig makes a suitable nose. For the mouth, drill a 1½" diameter hole, centered and 3" from the bottom.

2. Cut a 10" long slice lengthwise from the top of the body (neck) (diagram 1). Place the cut side against the back of the head, and nail in place with three pilot holes.

3. Arrange the pair of arms on the back, at a point 15" down from the chin. Nail the arms to the body from the back with pilot holes and two or three nails (diagram 2).

Diagram 2

Add vines for hair, or nail on an old straw hat. Dress as desired.

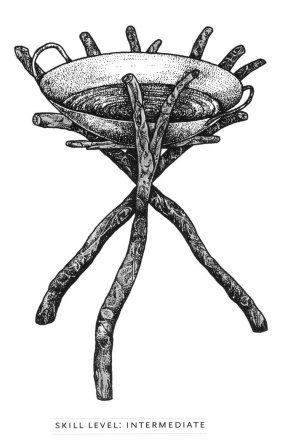

Birdbath Stand

*And we'd be as happy
as birds in the spring...*

WILLIAM BLAKE,
"THE LITTLE VAGABOND"

A BIRDBATH is a delightful addition to any garden and promises year-long enjoyment. This example, with its graceful proportions, is art for your garden. Use a sealed terra-cotta saucer, a discarded wok, or any shallow pan for the bath. For winter use, when birds need water for drinking, paint the inside of your birdbath with lead-free, flat black paint to stop the water from freezing and place in a sunny, windless area and fill with water. If the water in your birdbath does freeze, bring it indoors until it thaws out.

		DIAMETER	LENGTH	
CUTTING CHART				
NAME OF PART	QUANTITY	(INCHES)	(INCHES)	DESCRIPTION
Legs A	3	1½	42	forked, hardwood
Supports B	3	½–¾	16	hardwood

TOOLS

• Single bit axe for felling trees	• Crosscut hand saw
• Clippers	• Ruler or measuring tape
• Marking pencil	• Hammer
• Drill with a selection of bits	• Safety goggles
• Work gloves	

MATERIALS

Three forked branches (any hardwood), approximately 42" long and 1½" in diameter, are required for the legs, and three hardwood branches 16" long and ½" to ¾" in diameter will be needed for the supports. You will also need galvanized flathead nails in assorted sizes (#4p, #6p, and #8p) along with a handful of finishing nails.

DIRECTIONS

Cutting the Branches

1. Cut three 1½" diameter hardwood branches for the legs A, each 42" long.
2. Cut three ½" to ¾" diameter branches for the supports B, each 16" long.

Building the Base

Diagram 1

1. Check each of the three legs to make sure they will fit together in a pleasing arrangement just where the forks form. Try several compositions before deciding on your final design. If necessary, cut off any small branches that interfere.

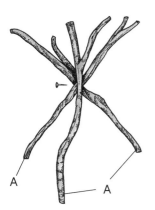

A

A

A

Diagram 2

2. Cross two legs at approximately 26" from the leg bottoms, forming an "X". Nail the two legs A together at this junction using a pilot hole.
3. Arrange the remaining leg, between the two joined legs through the top of the "X". Nail to the first two joined legs using a pilot hole.
4. Check for stability and adjust the ends, if necessary.

Adding the Supports
1. Drill a pilot hole approximately 4" from the end of one support B and through a point approximately 10" down from the top of one fork of a leg. Nail the support to the leg at this point. With the support horizontal, nail its other end to the adjacent leg.
2. The three supports B are attached under and over each other, forming an equilateral triangle. Nail the remaining two supports B over the first installed support and drilling a pilot hole first, nail them together.
3. Nail the supports to the legs at the locations where they meet (roughly horizontally) as shown in diagram 4.

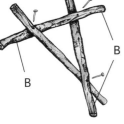

B

B

Diagram 3

Rest a clay saucer or any suitable vessel on the supports, allowing the extended legs to cradle it.

NOTE: To seal a terra-cotta saucer, apply several coats of marine varnish.

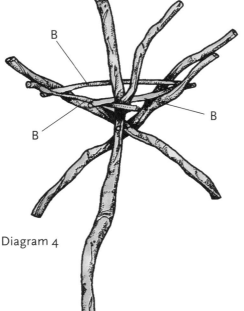

B

B

B

B

Diagram 4

Sundial
Stand

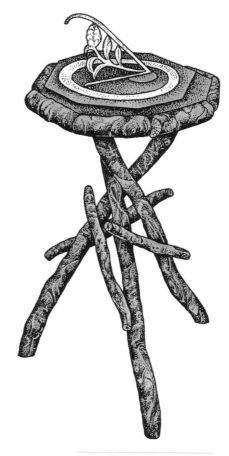

Stand on the highest pavement of the stair—
Lean on a garden urn—
Weave, weave the sunlight in your hair.

T.S. ELIOT

PLACE A PURCHASED sundial on this simple stand in the midst of your garden, and you will always know what time it is. Based on early Gypsy designs, this easy stand is a good beginners project that will add interest to your landscape. Ground-hugging plants like mother-of-thyme or purslane are lovely planted at the base. Sundials may be purchased at garden supply shops, some hardware stores, and in many gift and gardening mail-order catalogues.

227

CUTTING CHART

NAME OF PART	QUANTITY	DIAMETER (INCHES)	LENGTH (INCHES)	DESCRIPTION
Legs A	3	1	30	hardwood
Cross braces B	3	¾	12	hardwood
Edge trim C	4	1¼	4–5	hardwood split in half
Top	1	½-thick	12 × 12	see diagram 2

TOOLS

- Single bit axe for felling trees
- Clippers
- Marking pencil
- Hammer
- Work gloves
- Crosscut hand saw
- Ruler
- ⅜" variable-speed drill
- Safety goggles

4½" to 5" each facet

2"

2"   C   2"

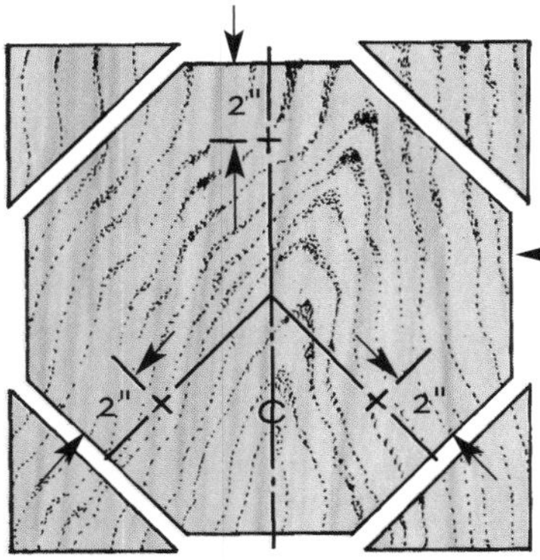

Diagram 1

MATERIALS

Alder, cedar, mulberry, willow, or other similar wood may be used. Lengths range from 4" to 30", and diameters from ¾" to 1¼". You will also need a ½" thick piece of plywood 1 ft. square for the top. #2p and #4p galvanized box nails are required (box nails are flathead nails, lighter in weight than common galvanized flathead nails).

DIRECTIONS

Making the Top

1. Cut ½" thick plywood in the octagonal shape as shown in diagram 1.
2. Place the top face down on the workbench. Using the pencil make three marks approximately 2" from the edge at the three loca-

tions indicated on the diagram. Drill pilot holes through the plywood at these marks to attach the legs.

3. Split the four edge trim C parts in half lengthwise, thereby creating eight pieces.
4. Arrange the edge trim C, with the split edge facing octagon table top edges. Drill and nail in place using two to three nails at each location.

Adding the Legs

Nail the three legs in place through the pilot holes in the table top. Legs cross at approximately 9" down forming the tripod. Nail them together at this point (diagram 2).

Adding the Cross Braces

1. Nail cross braces B, at a slant, between neighboring legs with pilot holes. See page 232 for placement.
2. Stand the table upright and check for stability. Adjust the leg bottoms, if necessary, by sawing the ends until the table is level.

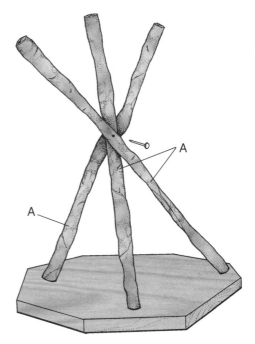

Diagram 2   Leg placement

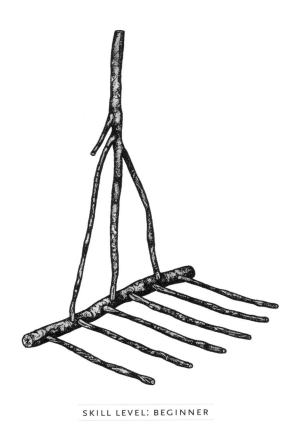

Hanging Herb & Flower Drying Rack

(Thymus vulgaris) Perennial. The green portion, either fresh or dried, is used extensively for flavoring soups, gravies, stews, etc. The leaves are easily dried in a shaded warm place. Pkt. 15 cts.

BURPEE'S ANNUAL FOR 1921

THIS SIMPLE hanging rack helps to preserve garden herbs, fruits, and flowers. For tea blends, cooking, flower arrangements, and crafts, dried herbs are essential. Pick the flowers to be preserved on a dry morning, after the dew has settled. Tie them in small bundles and hang them upside down away from direct sunlight. Some of the herbs that dry most successfully in this manner are dill, lovage, the mints, oregano, parsley, rosemary, sage, tarragon, and thyme.

CUTTING CHART

NAME OF PART	QUANTITY	DIAMETER (INCHES)	LENGTH (INCHES)	DESCRIPTION
Hanger A	1	¼–¾	22	3-forked/pliable
Support bar B	1	1	19	straight
Pegs C	6	¼–½	10–12	straight

TOOLS

- Single bit axe for felling trees
- Clippers or garden shears
- Marking pencil
- Hammer
- Work gloves

- Crosscut hand saw
- Ruler or measuring tape
- ⅜" variable-speed drill and a selection of bits
- Safety goggles

MATERIALS

You will want to choose straight but pliable branches of willow, alder, hickory, cedar, or another similar wood. Lengths will range from 10" to 21", and diameters from ¼" to 1". You will need one multi-forked branch for the hanger and a 1" diameter hardwood branch support bar. You will also need an assortment of galvanized finishing nails.

DIRECTIONS

Cutting the Branches

1. Cut one ¼" to ¾" diameter three-forked twig for the hanger A, 22" long.
2. Cut one 1" diameter straight stick for the support bar B, 19" long.
3. Cut six ¼" to ½" diameter straight twigs for the pegs C, each approximately 11" long.

Building the Rack

1. Position the three-forked hanger A, along the top of the support bar B. Mark the three points where the branches meet the support bar.
2. Using the drill and correct bit (with diameters to match those of the

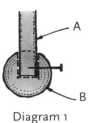

Diagram 1

forks) for the three-forked hanger A, drill three holes halfway through the support bar. Insert the hanger branches, and nail in place with finishing nails. This assures a secure fit (diagram 1).

3. Mark two points at 1½" in from each end of the support bar B; and then mark points, evenly spaced, approximately 3" apart. Carefully drill holes (halfway) for the correct peg diameters at these points (diagram 2).

4. Place the pegs snugly in the drilled holes. Use a dab of glue in the hole and a dab on the peg. If the peg fits loosely in the hole, dip the end in sawdust and then insert it. Allow the hanging rack to dry thoroughly before using.

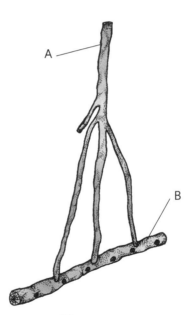

Diagram 2

Herb & Flower Drying Stand

Open afresh your round of starry folds,
Ye ardent marigolds.

JOHN KEATS

GATHER YOUR fresh herbs before the first frost, and hang them in bunches to dry on this standing rack. They will help to scent and decorate your kitchen and your seasonings will be close by. This adjustable rack folds up for out-of-season storage. Its unique design is composed of four separate sections that connect with metal screw-eyes from the hardware store.

233

		DIAMETER	LENGTH	
NAME OF PART	QUANTITY	(INCHES)	(INCHES)	DESCRIPTION
Legs A	5	¾–1	36	straight/hardwood
Rails B	12	½–¾	20	straight/hardwood

CUTTING CHART

TOOLS

• Single bit axe for felling trees	• Coping saw
• Crosscut hand saw	• Ruler
• Marking pencil	• Drill with a selection of bits
• Hammer	• Safety goggles
• Work gloves	

MATERIALS

You will need five ¾" to 1" diameter straight branches for the legs, each 3 ft. long; and twelve ½" to ¾" diameter straight branches for the rails, each 20" long. Nine 3" to 4" metal screw-eyes are required to join the sections, as well as an assortment of galvanized common nails.

DIRECTIONS

Cutting the Branches

1. Cut five ¾" to 1" diameter straight branches for the legs A, each 3 ft. long.
2. Cut twelve ½" to ¾" diameter straight branches for the rails B, each 20" long.

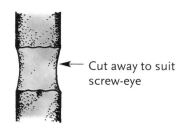

← Cut away to suit screw-eye

Diagram 1

Laying Out the Assembly

1. Lay all the legs A on the workbench. Using the pencil, make a mark 1 ft. from the bottom of each leg. As an aid to simplify construction, wrap a small piece of masking tape around each leg and label as follows: A1, A2, A, A3, and A4. Set these aside. NOTE: Before attaching the screw-eyes to the rails, make certain the screw-eyes are able to slip around the legs. If need be, cut away a bit of the leg to allow this to happen (diagram 1).

2. Place all of the rails B on the work-bench. Screw the 3" or 4" metal screw-eye through one end of each of the rails. To help with construction, as above, with masking tape on each part, label three rails B1, three rails B2, three rails B, and three rails B3. Set these aside.

NOTE: Refer to diagram 2 to understand the following steps.

3. Slip one screw-eye/B1 rail around leg A2 at the 1 ft. mark.
4. Fit the B1 rail against the A1 leg at the 1 ft. mark, and nail together using a pilot hole.
5. Place one screw-eye/B2 rail around leg A at the 1 ft. mark.
6. Fit the B2 rail against the A2 leg at a point just above the rail from step 3; nail to leg A2 with a pilot hole.
7. Fit the second B1 rail screw-eye part over leg A2 at a point approximately 11" up from the first B1 rail.
8. Using a pilot hole, nail the B1 rail to the A1 leg at a point 11" up from the first attached B1 rail.
9. Fit the second B2 rail screw-eye part over leg A at a point approximately 11" up from the first B2 rail.
10. Using a pilot hole, nail the B2 rail to the A2 leg at a point 11" up from the first attached B2 rail.
11. Add the last B1 rail screw-eye part over leg A2, 11" up from the previous attached rail.
12. Using a pilot hole, nail the B1 rail to the A1 leg 11" up from the last attached B1 rail.
13. Add the last B2 rail in the same manner as steps 9 and 10 above.

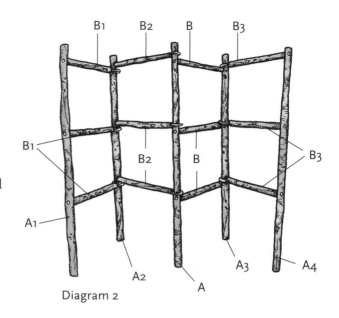

Diagram 2

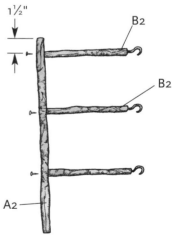

Diagram 3   Make two

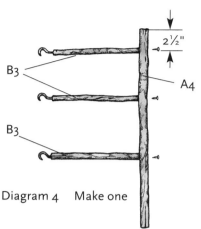

Diagram 4   Make one

Joining the Parts

1. At the 11" mark on leg A, at a point just below the bottom B2 screw-eye, butt bottom rail B against leg A and nail in place. Butt the same rail B, against leg A3 at the 11" mark; using a pilot hole, nail rail B to leg A3.
2. Slip screw-eye rail B3 over leg A3 just above installed B rail.
3. Butt bottom B3 rail against leg A4, and nail with a pilot hole (diagram 4).
4. Butt rail B against leg A, just below the middle installed rail B2, and nail to leg A and to leg A3 with a pilot hole (diagram 5).
5. Slip the middle screw-eye B3 rail over leg A3, just above the middle B rail.
6. Using a pilot hole, nail the B3 rail to leg A4 at a point 11" up from the first B3 rail.
7. Butt the remaining B rail against leg A, just below the top attached B2 rail; using a pilot hole, nail B to leg A just below the top B2 rail, and to leg A3 at approximately 11" above the center B rail.

Completing the Structure

1. Butt the bottom rail B3 against leg A4 at the 1 ft. mark, and nail with a pilot hole.
2. Repeat step 1 with the center rail B3 at a point 11" up; repeat with the remaining rail B3 at 11".
3. Slip the three extended screw-eye B3 rails over leg A3. They will sit just above the three installed rails B.

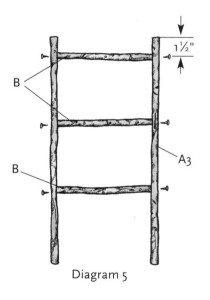

Diagram 5

NOTE: The sections should be able to move easily to allow for folding.

Mini Chair Plant Stand

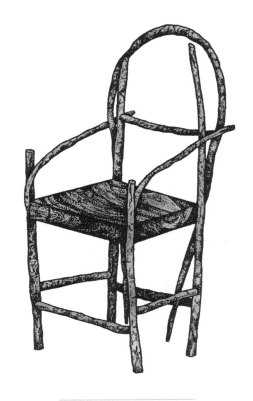

I have a garden of my own,
But so with roses overgrown,
And lilies that you would it guess
To be a little wilderness.

ANDREW MARVEL

THIS PINT-SIZE bentwood chair lends rustic charm wherever it is placed—on a kitchen shelf, a bedside stand, or a windowsill. A piece of scrap lumber, some willow twigs, and birch bark trim combine to create a platform for tiny plants or fresh cut flowers.

NAME OF PART	QUANTITY	DIAMETER (INCHES)	LENGTH (INCHES)	DESCRIPTION
Back legs A	2	½	13–14	straight
Front legs/arms B	2	½-legs; ¼-arms	8-legs; 7-arms	pliable/ forked
Front/back braces C	2	¼–½	4½-back; 5½-front	straight
Side braces D	2	¼–½	4¼	straight
Ladderback E	1	½	4½	straight
Bentwood back F	1	¼	31	pliable

T O O L S

• Clippers or garden shears	• Tack hammer
• Coping saw	• Ruler or measuring tape
• Marking pencil	• Scissors
• Carpenter's glue (white or yellow)	• Work gloves

MATERIALS

You will need pliable branches such as willow, alder, mulberry, or hickory. Lengths will range from 4" to 31", and branches should be ⅛" to ½" in diameter, including two matched forked branches to form the front legs/arms. ¾" thick wood scraps, 5½" × 6½", are required for the seats, along with 1" wide pieces of birch bark for trim. You will also need an assortment of finishing nails. The seat may be painted, if you so choose. There is a pattern provided for the seat.

DIRECTIONS

Cutting the Branches

1. Cut two ½" diameter branches for the back legs A, each approximately 14" long. NOTE: The length varies between 13" and 14", allowing for the natural crooks and bends on the twig.

2. Cut two forked branches for the front legs/arms B; the ½" diameter leg, 8" long; and the pliable ¼" diameter arm, 7" long.

3. Cut two ¼" to ½" diameter front/back braces C, 4½" long for the back and 5½" long for the front.

4. Cut two ¼" to ½" diameter side braces D, each 4½" long.

5. Cut one ½" diameter branch for the ladderback E, 4½" long.

6. Cut one ¼" diameter pliable branch for the bentwood back F, 31" long.

Building the Chair

NOTE: To use the pattern (diagram 1) make two copies on a photocopier (or trace two copies); turn one side over and tape together along the center line. Trace outline onto the 5½" × 6½" piece of wood.

1. Transfer the pattern onto the 5½" × 6½" piece of wood and cut out the seat, cutting the four corners to match the legs using a coping saw. NOTE: If you decide to paint the seat, do it now.

2. Position the back legs A in the seat back at the two corner cutouts. (The legs extend 7" below the seat corner.) Drill pilot holes and nail the two back legs A to the seat at the back corner cutout locations.

3. Position the front legs/arms B at the two front corner cutouts. (The legs extend 6¾" below the seat corners at the front.) Drill pilot holes and nail the two front legs B to the seat front at both corner cutout locations.

4. Carefully bend each extended arm toward the corresponding back leg.

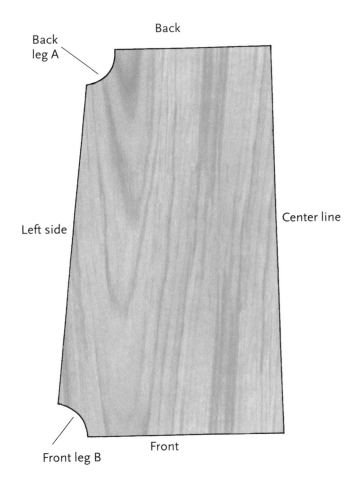

Diagram 1 Seat half-pattern (make two). Enlarge by 133% and then take copy and enlarge by a further 200%.

(The arm extends approximately 1½" beyond the back leg, and rests against the outside of the leg.) The ladderback E is butted between the back legs A at this junction. Drill a pilot hole completely through the arm, and the corresponding back leg at the location where they meet, and partway through the ends of the ladderback E. Nail all three parts together through the arms.

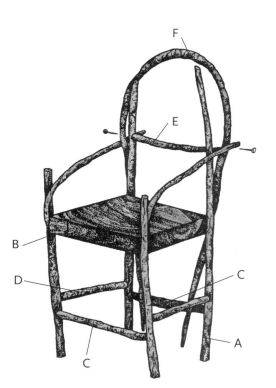

Diagram 2

5. Butt the 4½" long back brace C between the back legs 2" from the bottom of each leg. Nail in place through the sides of the legs.

6. Butt the 5½" long front brace C between the front legs at 2" from the bottom of each leg. Nail in place through the sides of the legs.

7. Butt the side braces D between the front and back legs at 2¾" from the bottom of each leg. Nail in place through the front and back of each leg.

8. Center the bentwood back F behind the back legs A, forming a hoop. Carefully bend the ends inside the bottom side braces D, and nail the bentwood part F to the seat. Once the bentwood hoop is dry it forms a tight fit against the extended back legs and between the extended arms. You may, however, decide to nail the hoop to the top of the legs before it dries.

Adding the Trim
Using the scissors, cut 1" wide strips of white birch bark to fit the seat edges. Glue them in place and allow to dry overnight.

Twig
Hanger

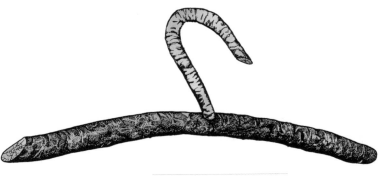

SKILL LEVEL: BEGINNER

Make sweet-scented bags of damask rose leaves,
lavender, and some cedar wood to lay with linen.

DENISE BENJAMIN, 1883

PICK UP STICKS and fashion them into useful natural hangers for hanging up gardening clothes, drying herbs in the kitchen, or dangling lavender sachets near the bath.

MATERIALS
Try to locate a hardwood branch such as white birch or cherry, with a slight bend for the arms, approximately 16" long and ¾" to 1" in diameter. You will also need a pliable twig, such as willow or alder, approximately 10" long and ½" in diameter for the hanger hook. You will require a piece of ¾" plywood and eight ½" common nails for forming the crook in the hanger hook, along with a dab of white glue to secure the hook in the arm. Pattern pieces are provided for the hook outline and hanger.

T O O L S	
• Crosscut hand saw	• Garden shears or clippers
• Ruler	• Pencil
• Drill with a selection of bits	

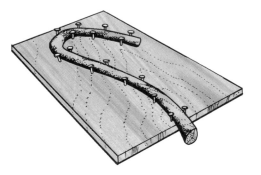

Diagram 1   Twig in the jig

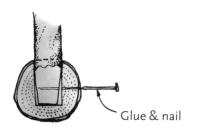

Glue & nail

Diagram 2

DIRECTIONS

1. Enlarge the hanger hook pattern by 50%. Draw the hanger hook outline on the plywood. Hammer in the nails so they stand upright. Arrange the pliable willow hanger hook along the nails. Allow it to dry (approximately 5 to 8 days).

2. Trim all protruding branches, and sand any rough edges on the hardwood branch. Trim and taper the ends, if needed.

3. When the hanger hook is completely dry, mark the location for the hook placement on the arm. Using a drill bit the same diameter as the end of the hook, drill partway through the hanger arm midway from each end. Fit the hook in the hole. When you are satisfied with the fit, add a dab of glue on the hook and in the hole. If it is loose in the hole, dip the end of the hook in sawdust before inserting it. "Lock" it in place with a small finishing nail (diagram 2). Allow it to dry overnight.

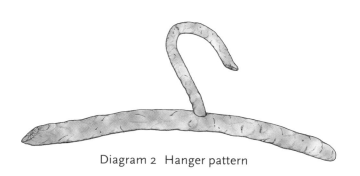

Diagram 2 Hanger pattern

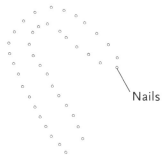

Nails

Hanger hook outline

Seed Caddies

How could such sweet and wholesome Hours,
Be reckon'd but with herbs and flow'rs!
ANDREW MARVELL

SEASONED GARDENERS often collect and save seeds from favorite heir-loom plants to sow the following season, or to share with friends. These easy-to-make containers are perfect for storing seeds, or even small trinkets.

T O O L S		

• Crosscut hand saw	• Ruler or measuring tape
• Marking pencil	• Tack hammer and tacks
• Sharp pocket knife for trimming the stoppers	• Sandpaper (optional)
• Vise for holding the branch steady while drilling	
• Electric drill with a 1⅜" bit, or a hand-held carpenter's auger	

MATERIALS

Choose hardwood branches such as white birch, maple, or cherry, approximately 3" in diameter for the containers, and approximately 1½" in diameter for the stoppers. The containers vary in height from 3" to 5", and the stoppers are 1½" to 2½" long. Tack on brown kraft paper recycled from grocery sacks for the paper labels.

DIRECTIONS

NOTE: Before the invention of the electric drill various tools were employed for boring different-size holes in wood, such as the nose auger, tap auger, or spoon bit. If you have an expansion bit and hand auger, try using it for this project. Using tools rather than machines may help develop a deeper relationship with your rustic work.

Making the Containers

1. Even out the bottom of the branches so they stand firmly upright. Measure and mark the center top of each branch. NOTE: Precautions should

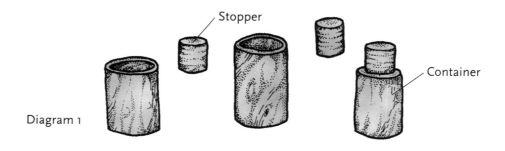

Stopper

Container

Diagram 1

be taken when drilling into the center of a branch. NEVER hold the small branch in your hand while drilling, and if you place a round branch in the jaws of a vise to hold it steady, you will probably crush it or at least mar the bark. A simple woodworking solution is to wrap the branch with a soft, dense fabric before placing it in the vise. An old towel, or scrap of terry cloth works very well.

2. Using the correct size bit, drill a hole at the center mark of each branch. For a 3" diameter branch, make the opening 2" in diameter, therefore leaving a 1" rim remaining. For a 3" tall branch, drill the hole 1½" deep leaving a 1½" bottom.

Making the Stoppers
Cut 1½" diameter branches 1½" to 2½" long. Lightly sand the cut edges. Plug the stoppers into the container openings, and use a sharp knife to adjust the fit if necessary. Fill with seeds and tack on labels.

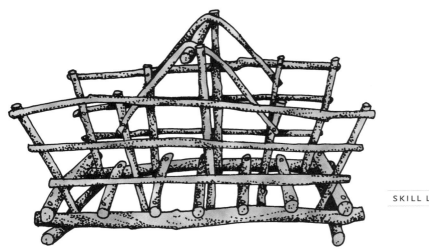

Herb Gathering Basket

Lean on a garden urn. Weave
weave the sunlight in your hair.

T.S. ELIOT,
"LA FIGLIA CHE PIANGE"

NOTHING COULD BE more suitable for gathering fresh herbs from the garden than this airy, rustic basket, fashioned out of straight willow branches. This is an excellent beginner project—perfect for the woodworker with limited space. Its open design protects delicate herbs from bruising, yet it is sturdy enough to carry home an ample supply for year-round cooking and preserving. It would also be a pretty stand-in centerpiece on a dining table holding pots of herbs, or on a winter mantel with evergreen boughs and pine cones.

CUTTING CHART

NAME OF PART	QUANTITY	DIAMETER (INCHES)	LENGTH (INCHES)	DESCRIPTION
Side staves A	4	½–¾	8	straight
Front & back staves B	2	½–¾	16	straight
Bottom C	5	¼–½	8	straight
Vertical supports D	8	¼–½	7	straight
Handle supports E	2	½	9	straight
Sides F	6	¼–½	13–15	straight
Handle G	1	½	9	straight
Handle trim H	2	¼	11	pliable

TOOLS

- Crosscut hand saw
- Ruler or measuring tape
- Drill and a selection of bits
- Safety goggles

- Clippers or garden shears
- Marking pencil
- Hammer and nails
- Work gloves

MATERIALS

You will need a selection of ¼" to ¾" diameter hardwood twigs, ranging in length from 8" to 15", along with finishing nails.

DIRECTIONS

Cutting the Branches

1. Cut four ½" to ¾" diameter branches, 8" long for the side staves A.
2. Cut two ½" to ¾" diameter branches, 16" long for the front and back staves B.
3. Cut five ¼" to ½" diameter branches, 8" long for the bottom C.
4. Cut four ¼" to ½" diameter branches, 7" long for the vertical supports D.
5. Cut two ½" diameter branches, 9" long for the handle supports E.
6. Cut six ¼" to ½" diameter branches in the following lengths: two 13" long, two 14" long, and two 15" long for the sides F.

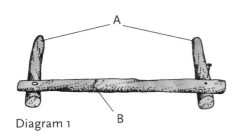

Diagram 1

7. Cut one ½" diameter branch, 9" long for the handle G.
8. Cut two pliable ¼" diameter branches, 11" long for the handle trim H.

Building the Bottom

1. Begin by laying two parallel side staves A down on the work surface. Lay one front stave B across the ends of the two parallel side staves. Nail in place (diagram 1).
2. Repeat on back stave B.
3. Lay one side stave C across the front and back staves at one end. Nail in place.
4. Repeat at the opposite end.
5. Arrange the five bottom branches D, across the two parallel staves B, spacing them approximately 2½" apart (diagram 2).

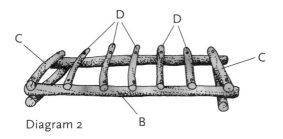

Diagram 2

Building the Sides

1. Place a vertical support E inside the bottom staves C, touching both side staves A. Drill and nail in place (diagram 3).
2. Repeat with three vertical supports E, at the three remaining corners.
3. Arrange the four remaining supports E inside the staves B (diagram 3), and using pilot holes, nail in place.
4. Arrange the handle support F inside the stave B, and nail it in place. Repeat with the opposite side.
5. Lay the construction on its side on the work surface. Arrange one 13" side branch F, across the vertical supports. Drill and nail in place.

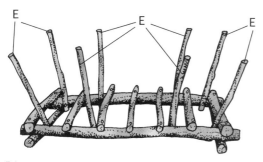

Diagram 3

6. Repeat with the remaining 14" and 15" side branches G, spacing them approximately 2" apart (diagram 4).

7. Turn the construction over, and repeat steps 5 and 6 above.

Adding the Handle

1. Overlap the handle H across both vertical handle supports F. Drill and nail in place.

2. Gently bend one pliable handle trim I. Place one end of I against the outside of one of the vertical supports E. Drill and nail in place, then arch it over and bring it down along the vertical support E on the opposite side. Drill and nail in place where I meets E (diagram 5).

3. Using the same method as above, nail the remaining handle trim I in place.

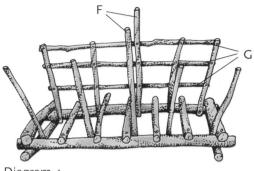

Diagram 4

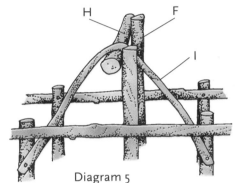

Diagram 5

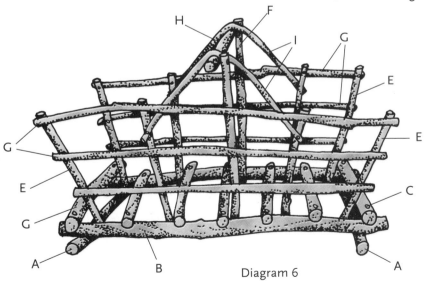

Diagram 6

May Baskets

*All in the merry month of May
when young buds they were swellin...*

ANONYMOUS

THE ARRIVAL of May has been celebrated since ancient times as the coming of spring. These baskets will help to revive a delightful old May Day custom of surprising a neighbor by hanging a basket of posies on his or her doorknob, and running away before anyone answers. Try your hand at either the whimsical willow and grapevine basket or the simple folded bark pocket. Both are good beginner projects. Place a clear glass jelly jar, or tin container inside the basket to hold water and fresh flowers. To attach the basket to the doorknob, loop and twist a wire around the handle.

T O O L S

- Garden shears or clippers
- Wire clippers
- For Bark Pocket: Ice pick or awl (or heavy twine and large-eyed needle)
- Pencil and ruler
- Scissors (for cutting bark)

MATERIALS

For the Willow and Grapevine Basket: You will need ¼" diameter pliable willow shoots, approximately 40" long, and a selection of young, very green flexible grapevine. Use green florist wire (26-gauge) to secure the basket spokes.

For the Folded Bark Pocket: You will need peeled birch bark, approximately 8" × 13", and a ⅛" to ¼" diameter flexible willow shoot, 30" long for the handle. Use two brass paper fasteners (or 28-gauge wire and two buttons) to secure the pocket.

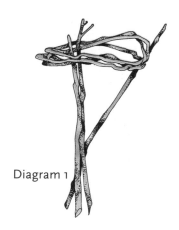

Diagram 1

DIRECTIONS

Willow and Grapevine Basket

NOTE: The following directions are for a 5" diameter basket.

1. Begin by making a 5" diameter willow wreath. To make the wreath, carefully bend a length of flexible willow into a circle, wrapping and twisting the two pliable ends over each other in a wreath shape.
2. Fit three 11" straight willow twigs (spokes), evenly spaced, through the wreath (diagram 1).
3. To make the handle, take one end of the 30" willow shoot and tuck it through the wreath, bringing it down to the ends of the 11" twigs. Gently bend it to form the handle. Tuck in the other end in the same manner. This will add two more spokes to the basket. Approximately 3" from the ends of the five spokes, use the wire to wrap them together (see diagram 2).
4. Weave the grapevine under and over the willow spokes until completed. NOTE: Wrap flexible willow or grapevine around the wire tie.

Diagram 2

DIRECTIONS

Folded Bark Pocket

Use a pencil to mark the bark, and cut it to size with scissors. Fold the birch bark sheet into the pocket shape. Hold the pocket steady with one hand while you secure it with brass fasteners through two pieces of bark, as pictured in diagram 3. NOTE: To close the pocket with buttons, use the awl or ice pick to make a hole in the bark. Use a piece of wire like a needle and thread to "sew" a button in place through the hole (diagram 4). Gently bend a 30" long flexible willow twig to form the handle. Tuck in the sides of the pocket, as pictured in diagram 5. Use heavy twine and a large-eyed needle, or an awl and wire to lace the handle to the pocket.

Diagram 3

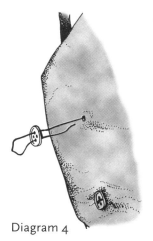

Diagram 4

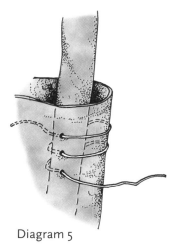

Diagram 5

Picnic
Cover

SKILL LEVEL: INTERMEDIATE

Tomatoes: and I love them, the love apples…
The best way to eat them is in the garden,
Warm and pungent from the vine…

M.F.K. FISHER,
"WITH BOLD KNIFE AND FORK"

PICNICS WITH PANACHE! Some designs cannot be improved upon, and this utilitarian picnic cover is a fine example of just such a functional project. For dining outdoors you will probably want to include more than one of these heirloom quality handcrafted food domes. Reinvented in bent willow and window screen, this version is reminiscent of early tin classics that were used to protect salads, sandwiches, and desserts from flying pests. Be prepared to take orders for these handy covers once you place them on your garden party table.

253

CUTTING CHART			
NAME OF PART	QUANTITY	DIAMETER (INCHES)	LENGTH (INCHES) DESCRIPTION
Base ring A	1	¼–½	95 pliable
Ribs B	3	¼	28 pliable

TOOLS	
• Clippers or garden shears	• Ruler or measuring tape
• Marking pencil	• Drill and a selection of bits
• Hammer and ¾" finishing nails	• Safety goggles and work gloves
• Wire cutter or tin snips for cutting the screen	

MATERIALS

You will need a selection of ¼" diameter pliable twigs, 28" long, and one ¼" to ½" diameter pliable twig, approximately 95" long. You will also need ¾" finishing nails and six pieces of wire screen approximately 9" × 12" each to complete the project. You may want to use approximately a dozen spring-type clothespins to temporarily hold the screen sections in place while you proceed with the project. You will also need wire cutting shears, a black marker, and 28-gauge silver beading wire (available at beading stores and some craft stores). NOTE: Use the silver wire for aluminum screen and copper wire for copper screen. A pine cone, button, or wood ring will work to make the finial.

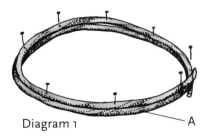

Diagram 1

DIRECTIONS

Cutting the Branches

1. Cut one ¼" to ½" diameter pliable branch, 95" long for the base ring A.
2. Cut three ¼" diameter pliable branches, 28" long for the ribs B.

Assembling the Twig Parts

1. Carefully bend the base ring branch A into a 14" diameter ring. NOTE: The branch is long enough

to go around twice. Using pilot holes drilled from the bottom, nail the branch together into a single ring (diagram 1).

2. Gently bend one rib part B into an arc shape. Place one end of part B along the outside of the base ring and nail from the front using a pilot hole. Place the remaining end on the opposite side and attach in the same fashion (diagram 2).

3. Repeat with the two remaining ribs, keeping them equally spaced: approximately 8" apart.

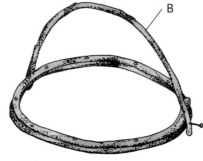

Diagram 2

Adding the Screen

NOTE: Because the size and shape of each section varies slightly, add the screen one section at a time between two ribs. Making a paper pattern for each section is an option, but not necessary.

Work gloves are essential when cutting screen.

1. Lay the dome down on its side on the work table. Working from the inside, arrange one piece of screen in one section. Use a 7" length of wire to attach the screen to the top of the ribs at the point where they cross at the center of the dome. Twist the wire to secure the screen and allow the extra length to remain. You will use the extended pieces of wire to attach the finial when all the sections are completed (diagram 3).

2. To obtain the exact size for each section, carefully press the screen against both ribs. You can use spring-type clothespins at this step to hold the screen in place. Trace the ribs with a marker to obtain the pie-shaped wedge on the screen. Cut the screen section to size with tin snips.

3. Use the silver wire to attach the screen section to the ribs and to the base at a few strategic loca-

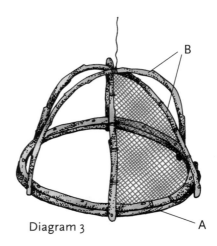

Diagram 3

Diagram 4

tions. NOTE: Insert both ends of the wire through the screen from the front, around the rib, and twist lightly along the inside of the dome.

4. Repeat steps 1, 2, and 3 above with the remaining five sections. Use the six extended wires to attach the finial to the top (diagram 4).